A
BANGKOK

Sketches of the city's architectural treasures...

Journey through Bangkok's urban landscape

Gregory Byrne Bracken

mc **Marshall Cavendish**
Editions

All text and illustrations by G. Byrne Bracken
Designer: Benson Tan

© 2016 Marshall Cavendish International (Asia) Private Limited

Published by Marshall Cavendish Editons
An imprint of Marshall Cavendish International
Times Centre, 1 New Industrial Road, Singapore 536196
Tel: (65) 6213 9300. E-mail: genref@sg.marshallcavendish.com
Online Bookstore: www.marshallcavendish.com/genref

Other Marshall Cavendish offices
Marshall Cavendish Corporation. 99 White Plains Road, Tarrytown NY 10591-9001,
USA • Marshall Cavendish International (Thailand) Co Ltd. 253 Asoke, 12th Flr,
Sukhumvit 21 Road, Klongtoey Nua, Wattana, Bangkok 10110, Thailand •
Marshall Cavendish (Malaysia) Sdn Bhd, Times Subang, Lot 46, Subang Hi-Tech
Industrial Park, Batu Tiga, 40000 Shah Alam, Selangor Darul Ehsan, Malaysia

Marshall Cavendish is a trademark of Times Publishing Limited

National Library Board (Singapore) Cataloguing in Publication Data
Names: Byrne Bracken, G. (Gregory)
Title: A walking tour Bangkok : sketches of the city's architectural treasures ... journey
through Bangkok's urban landscape / Gregory Byrne Bracken.
Other titles: Bangkok : a walking tour.
Description: Third edition. | Singapore : Marshall Cavendish Editions, [2016] | Includes
bibliographical references and index.
Identifiers: OCN 935266957 | ISBN 978-981-47-2178-3 (paperback)
Subjects: LCSH: Walking—Thailand—Bangkok—Guidebooks. | Historic buildings—
Thailand—Bangkok—Guidebooks. | Historic sites—Thailand—Bangkok—Guidebooks. |
Architecture—Thailand—Bangkok--Guidebooks. | Bangkok (Thailand—Tours. | Bangkok
(Thailand)—Guidebooks.
Classification: LCC DS589.B2 | DDC 915.93—dc23

Printed in Singapore by Fabulous Printers Pte Ltd

Contents

Acknowledgments

I would like to thank everyone who has helped me with this book, particularly Melvin Neo, Justin Lau and Benson Tan at Marshall Cavendish for their wonderful support.

Suggested Itineraries

History
Charoen Krung Road
Rattanakosin
Bang Lamphoo
Dusit District

Culture
Rattanakosin
Dusit District
Further Afield

Markets
Prathunam
Silom Road
Charoen Krung Road
Chinatown
Bang Lamphoo
Further Afield (Chatuchak Weekend Market)

Shopping
Prathunam
Wireless Road
Silom Road
Charoen Krung Road
Chinatown

Children's
Prathunam
Dusit District

Introduction

Bangkok is notorious for its traffic, which means that walking is one of the best ways of getting around the city. It is also greener than most people realise with a number of different areas, almost cities within a city, which are best explored on foot.

Each chapter of this book shows a suggested walking route, each following on from where the previous one left off. These try to cover one particular area per walk, like Chinatown or Rattanakosin, but the city's Downtown is so large that it has been split into three separate walks. Distances can be huge, city blocks in Bangkok are big and have few crossing streets, the advantage is that once you're on the road you'll have less chance of missing the things you want to see. The buildings and sites listed are only suggestions for visiting, they don't have to be followed rigorously, and apart from the usual temples, mosques, churches and museums there's also information on other places of interest, like skyscrapers which have restaurants, bars or galleries with good views of the city.

Be careful when following some of the routes as Bangkok can be treacherous — uneven paving, crumbling edges, even gaping holes that are left unprotected — so watch your step, particularly when you have your eyes gazing upward at the buildings. Remember to stop often, don't overdo it in the tropical weather. Drink plenty of liquids, and there are numerous shops, cafes and restaurants en route to stop in and rest. Parts of Bangkok can be surprisingly green, with shady trees lining the roadways, but increasingly shadows seem to be coming from the increasingly tall buildings in and around the city.

Most of Bangkok's streets are lively day and night, and there's nearly always something interesting to see, and smell or even taste, so enjoy the experience. Do remember, however, that if you want to go into places like temples and some museums you must dress appropriately (i.e. you can't wear shorts, tee-shirts or sandals).

Monk and friend

Notes

A Note on History

After a particularly savage attack by the Burmese in 1767, Auytthaya, the capital of Siam (as the Kingdom of Thailand was then known), was destroyed. It had been the country's capital for more than four centuries and had been as large and rich as many European cities. The site was now considered too vulnerable and so a new capital was founded by King Taksin farther down the Menam River at Thonburi. A short time later the King went mad and was overthrown by one of his generals, Phraya Chakri, who put him to death. Phraya Chakri then took the title Rama I and founded the Chakri dynasty, which still reigns today, King Bumibol (pronounced Bumibon) is known as Rama IX.

> **Did You Know?**
> King Taksin was executed in the prescribed way for Thai royalty, by being tied up in a velvet sack and beaten to death with a sandalwood club.

Rama I then moved the capital, which was known to Westerners as Bancok, or the village of the wild plum, to the more easily defended eastern side of the river, forcing the Chinese merchants who had settled there to move farther downstream to what is present-day Chinatown. He built a series of defensive canals, a palace and a new temple to house the Emerald Buddha. He called the new 'Royal Island' Rattanakosin, but the name Bangkok stuck in Westerners' minds. At Rama I's coronation in 1782 he renamed the new capital Khrung Thep Phra Maha Nakhorn (the City of Angels, the Capital City), and it is still known to Thais as Khrung Thep (City of Angels) a shortened form of what has since become the longest city name in the world.

Until the second half of the twentieth century the main means of transport in the city was by boat, and though a lot of the canals, known as *khlongs*, have since been culverted, it still remains one of the best ways to see Bangkok. Filling in the canals wasn't just an aesthetic impoverishment, the waterways had acted as drains for the entire delta and their loss has left the city more prone to flooding than ever, but it didn't do enough to alleviate the road shortage anyway. The Chao Phraya River, which changed its name from the Menam in honour of Rama I, is teeming with craft, from huge cargo barges to ferries and longtail boats, and is the backbone of a network of canals, which in Thonburi are still relatively intact and give a flavour of what Bangkok life used to be like.

Towards the end of the nineteenth century, Rama V relocated the royal family to the Dusit district in the north of the city, where he constructed impressive avenues, palaces and temples, while the area around Sathorn

Map of Thailand

CHINA

VIETNAM

MYANMAR

LAOS

THAILAND

Bangkok

CAMBODIA

MALAYSIA

0   500 km

N

and Silom Roads became a fashionable enclave for rich foreigners who built gracious villas overlooking the wide roads and tree-lined canals.

The second half of the twentieth century saw uncontrolled urban expansion, particularly to the east. Bangkok in 1900 was about 13 square kilometres, but by 1980 had ballooned to 330 square kilometres, and it is still growing. Earlier attempts at orderly planning were obliterated and the city now has a series of different centres; from Rattanakosin and Chinatown, to the area between Silom Road and Prathunam, and even Sukhumvit Road. But if the visitor is prepared to explore, the city can be very rewarding, with pockets of charm in the oddest places, from serene temples, to lush parks, and even little corners of traditional activity that still take place much as they must have done in the days of Rama I.

Note: Siam

When Field Marshall Phibul became Prime Minister of Siam in 1939 he changed the name to Muang Thai (Land of the Thai), even though it is more commonly called Prathet Thai (Kingdom of the Thai) by the Thais themselves, and almost exclusively Thailand, an odd mix of Thai and English, by the rest of the world. It was done partly to try and break the Chinese stranglehold on the Thai economy (the overseas Chinese here are less visible than in other Southeast Asian countries, but their influence is still considerable), and to lay claim to territory housing Thai people which had been lost to the neighbouring French and British colonial empires over the previous decades. By allying themselves with Japan during World War II Thailand hoped to regain what had been unjustly wrested from them, in this they were unsuccessful, but like other politically motivated name changes, Ceylon (Sri Lanka), Irian Jaya (New Guinea), Burmah (Myanmar), Siam has perhaps lost something in the translation.

Note: Loy Krathong Festival

One of Thailand's best-loved national festivals pays homage to Mae Khong Kha, the goddess of rivers and waterways. In the evenings of the full moon during the 12th lunar month (November), people gather at rivers, lakes and ponds to float *krathongs*, which are small lotus-shaped baskets containing flowers, incense and candles. The festival originated in the north of Thailand and places like Chiang Mai and particularly Sukhothai are still the best places to see it today.

A Note on Climate

Bangkok's climate is governed by three seasons: the cool season, running from November to February, is the pleasantest time to visit, temperatures average around 27 degrees; the hot season, beginning in March, with highs of up to 37 degrees; and the rainy season, which varies from year to year, but usually starts in May and reaches a climax in September or October, with

Bangkok Districts

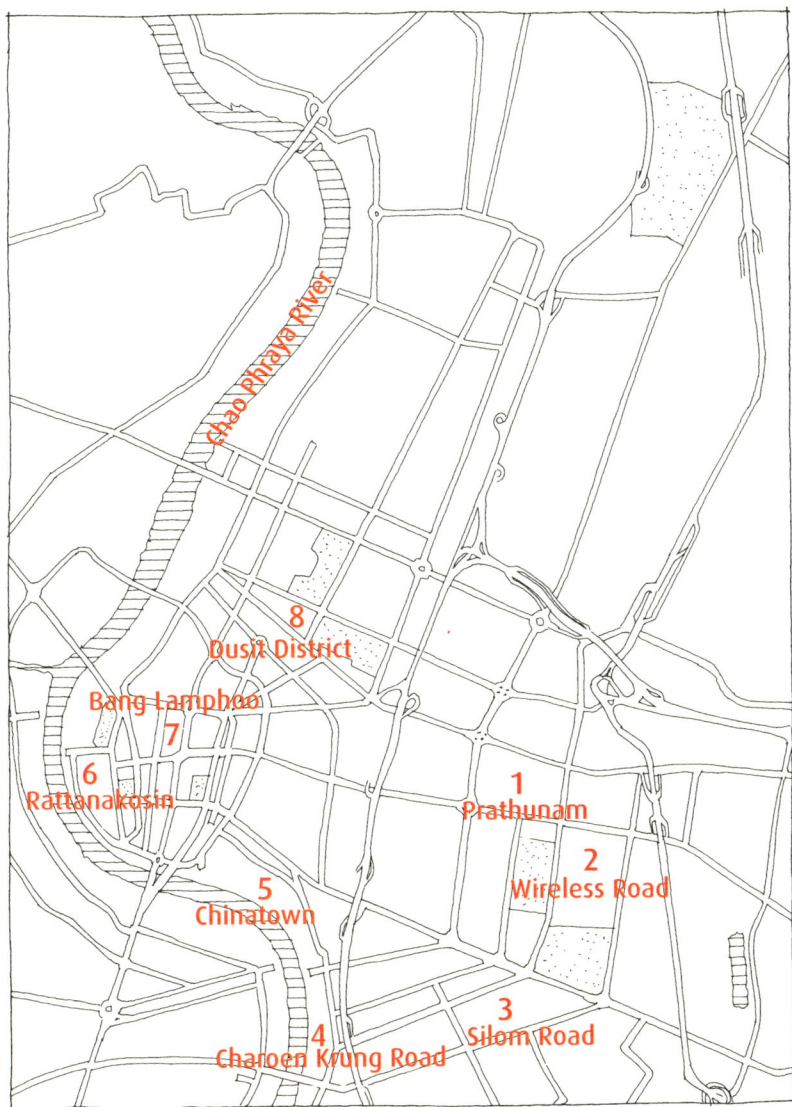

Chao Phraya River

8
Dusit District

Bang Lamphoo

7

6
Rattanakosin

1
Prathunam

2
Wireless Road

5
Chinatown

3
Silom Road

4
Charoen Krung Road

0   2.5 km

eighty per cent of the annual rainfall occurring during the late afternoon showers, which are often accompanied by spectacular thunder and lightning.

A Note on Spelling
Spellings differ in Bangkok, on maps, in guides and even from place to place. Those in this guide are standardised with a mind to simple, clear pronunciation.

A Note on Icons
To inform readers about the interesting features of the places they pass, we have added icons, drawn by the author, to represent the following:

Must See

National Monument

Good View

See At Night

Drinking

Eating

Shopping

A Note on Dress
You should dress comfortably for the tropics, but remember that in Thailand you should also cover up your body as much as possible. You will not be allowed into places such as temples wearing short trousers or short-sleeved shirts. Shoes must be removed before entering certain buildings, temples mainly, but some homes and offices will expect you to do so as well, basically if you see a pile of shoes at or near an entrance, you should remove your own as well before entering.

Note on Social Behaviour

Thais address people by their first name, usually with the word '*khun*' in front of it, which is used for both males and females. Thais rarely shake hands, using the traditional form of greeting known as the '*wai*' to say hello, goodbye, thank you and to apologise. As complex in its social ramifications as the Japanese bow, the *wai* is a prayer-like gesture made with palms pressed together in front of the chest, nose or forehead. Feel free to imitate one if someone *wais* to you — any clumsiness will be forgiven — but it's best not to initiate one as it can be embarrassing, particularly for the Thais. Never raise your voice or allow yourself to seem angry, you'll be even less likely to achieve your objectives — Thais avoid confrontation at all costs. Pointing your feet at anyone is considered rude, so be careful how you sit, especially if you're crossing your legs, never put your feet on a table. In temples, make sure you sit with your feet tucked away from the sacred images. Public displays of physical affection, other than innocent ones between friends such as hand-holding, are generally frowned upon.

A Note on Taboos

Monks are revered in Thailand, and most Thai men spend at least some part of their lives in a monastery. Most taboos to do with monks concern women, who are not allowed to touch a monk, or directly hand anything to one. The royal family is not only revered but is genuinely loved. Criticising or defaming them will not only be crass and offensive, but can, under certain circumstances, be considered a crime. Because the Thai currency bears the king's image, you must treat it with respect, and if you happen to be anywhere and they start to play the National Anthem, follow the lead of the Thais around you and stand to attention.

Checklist

Sunglasses.
Sunscreen.
A small umbrella for the frequent showers. It can also come in useful as a parasol.
A small hand towel.
A small bottle of something to drink is essential.
Tiger Balm, when applied promptly to mosquito bites is extremely effective in preventing them from itching and becoming inflamed.

"Bangkok is the most hokum place I have ever seen, never having been to California. It is a triumph of the 'imitation' school; nothing is what it looks like; if it is not parodying European buildings it is parodying Khmer ones; failing anything else it will parody itself."

— Geoffrey Gorer, *Bali and Angkor*

Prathunam

Nearest Skytrain Station: National Stadium
Approximate walking time: 1 hour 30 minutes

Downtown North

Prathunam means 'water gate' in Thai and refers to the canal lock which used to be located on Khlong San Sap here. This area is home to an interesting mix of buildings, old and new, iincluding Jim Thompson's famous Thai-style house, some stylish new shopping centres, and the Baiyoke Tower II, the tallest building in Thailand.

THE WALK

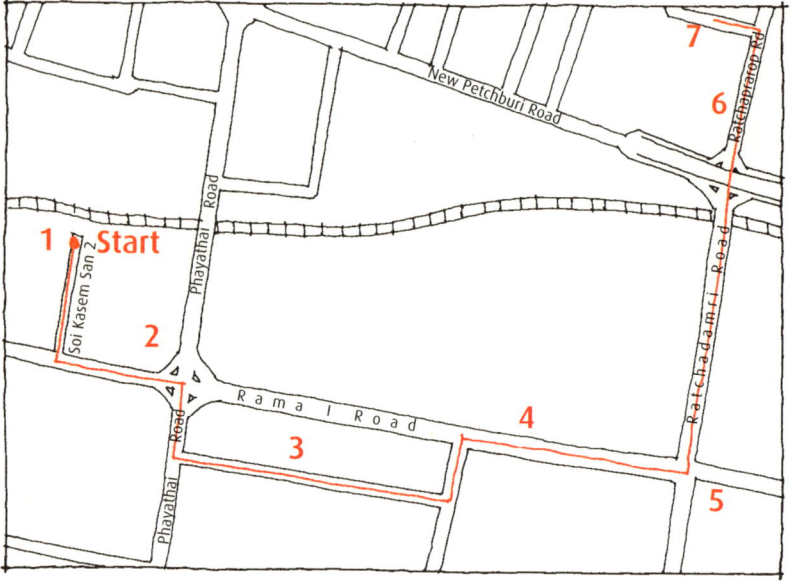

KEY

1. Jim Thompson's House
2. Bangkok Art and Culture Centre
3. Siam Square
4. Wat Pathum Wanaram
5. Erawan Shrine
6. Prathunam Market
7. Baiyoke Tower II

prathunam

Jim Thompson's House

If you are walking from the National Stadium Skytrain Station, follow Rama I Road away from the direction of Phayathai Road and turn right into Soi Kasem San 2. Jim Thompson's House will be on your left at the end of this narrow laneway. Thompson was instrumental in reviving the Thai silk industry after World War II. In 1958, he bought a traditional Thai house, dismantled it and rebuilt in the centre of the compound and added to it using a number of other tradition houses found in Ayutthaya. They were reconstructed using traditional methods (wooden pegs, no nails) but follow an unconventional plan, with some of the walls turned inside out to better highlight their craftsmanship. The deep red colour of the exteriors is unusual and is the result of wood preservative and has nothing to do with Thai traditional style, although it is very striking.

The small garden is densely planted and overlooks a narrow stretch of the busy Khlong San Sap which used to be a centre of silk weaving. Thompson was a knowledgeable collector of Southeast Asian art and antiquities and the house contains some fine stone carvings, Buddha heads and traditional Thai paintings. There is an easy informality to the whole place, it's almost as if Thompson has just popped out for a moment, in fact he disappeared without

Jim Thompson's House

trace in Malaysia in 1967. Access to the house is via guided tour. There is also a bar and restaurant, as well as a gift shop.

Jim Thompson's House
Opening times: 9am to 5pm daily.
Admission charges.

Note: Jim Thompson
Born in Delaware, USA in 1906, Jim Thompson had worked as an architect in New York before coming to Thailand in 1945 as the Bangkok head of the Office of Strategic Services, an early version of the CIA. In 1948 he founded the Thai Silk Company Ltd and almost single-handedly revived an ailing industry. He then disappeared quite suddenly in Malaysia's Cameron Highlands in 1967. Some maintain he got lost in the jungle, not a particularly pleasant way to die, but rumours persist that there was CIA involvement, the fact that his sister was murdered in the USA the previous year didn't help. The most likely theory, if a little mundane, is that he was knocked down by a car or lorry and his body buried to cover up the accident.

Bangkok Art and Culture Centre

Retrace your steps down Soi Kasem San 2 until you emerge onto Rama I Road and turn left. You will see the Bangkok Art and Culture Centre on your left overlooking the junction with Phayathai Road. This stark looking temple to culture sits hemmed in by shopping centres and represents a victory for

Bangkok Art and Culture Centre

Siam Paragon

SIAM PARAGON

Bracken

Bangkok's artistic community who had to battle to prevent the site being used for yet another commercial venture.

Inspired by the Guggenheim Museum in New York, it was built in 2008 and contains an airy atrium criss-crossed by escalators and lined with sloping walkways. Home to exhibition and performance spaces, there are also meeting rooms, a library and study area, and a café.

Bangkok Art and Culture Centre
Opening times: 10am to 9pm, Tue-Sun
Admission: free

Siam Square

Diagonally across the junction of Rama I and Phayathai Roads sits Siam Square. This isn't a square in the usual sense but actually a grid of small sois between Chulalongkorn University and Rama I Road. Located just opposite the Siam Centre, one of Thailand's first shopping centres, and beside a number of popular cinemas, this open-air square is packed with small shops and stalls selling music, books, accessories and clothing. A number of young Thai designers also sell their work here. This area has become something of a new city centre of sorts, being the Skytrain interchange. Across Rama I Road from Siam Square sit a number of upmarket shopping centres, including the older **Siam Centre** as well as the newer **Siam Discovery Centre** and **Siam Paragon** complexes. Siam Paragon is also home to **Siam Ocean World**, a massive aquarium, which is a huge attraction, especially at weekends for families with children. There is the obligatory underwater tunnel as well as a massive eight-metre-deep tank for coral reef as well as a smaller tank where visitors can actually touch sea creatures such as starfish.

Siam Ocean World
Opening times: 9am to 10pm daily
Admission Charges

Note: Skytrain

Elevated on a pre-stressed concrete viaduct supported by massive columns supporting spans of anything from 35 to 60 metres, the Bangkok Skytrain follows two of the city's main arterial routes, Silom and Sukhumvit Roads, transforming certain parts of them into sunless chasms. Delightfully, the new elevated public spaces which have been created on the 23 station platforms 12 metres above street level reveal Bangkok to be a far greener city than is at first apparent. With an average travelling speed of 35 kilometres per hour (or three times faster than the usual pace of cars in the city), the Skytrain indeed makes for a convenient and pleasant way to get around.

Wat Pathum Wanaram

Leave Siam Square by turning right onto Rama I Road and you will come to Wat Pathum Wanaram on your left after the junction with Henri Dunant Road. This temple, with its delightful cluster of buildings asymmetrically arranged among mature trees and shrubs, and sitting overlooking a small canal, is unlike any of the others in the city. It does not feel urban or hemmed in despite opening onto a busy road and being overlooked by the Skytrain and surrounding skyscrapers. Originally planned by Rama IV in the 1850s as a

Wat Pathum Wanaram

royal pleasure garden, it was known as the Lotus Pond (Sra Pathum) and contained a private place of worship for the king. Now it is home to the Phra Meru Mas, a reconstruction of the Princess Mother's crematorium and supposed to represent Mount Meru, the mythical home of the gods. It is a rare example of ancient craftsmanship, featuring ornate stencils and lacquered sculptures. Following the Princess Mother's cremation at Sanam Luang in 1996 her remains were transferred here in an elaborate procession. She was particularly revered, for although being born a commoner she was the mother of two kings, Rama VIII and his brother, the current king, Rama IX.

Wat Pathum Wanaram
Opening times: 8:30am to 6pm daily
Admission: free

Erawan Shrine

Continue along Rama I Road and the Erawan Shrine will be diagonally across the busy junction with Ratchadamri Road. This garish L-shaped shrine is one of the best known in the city, mainly because of its prominent location on a

Erawan Shrine

Prathunam

busy corner outside the Grand Hyatt Erawan Hotel. It dates from the 1950s when a number of accidents occurred while building the hotel (the foundation stone had been laid on an inauspicious day), so it was decided to build a shrine to Brahma and Erawan (his elephant mount) to try and appease the bad spirits. The accidents stopped and the shrine rapidly gained a reputation as a place to seek divine intercession.

Busy day and night, the faithful come to light incense and pray, and they often pay the colourfully dressed temple dancers to perform in thanksgiving for prayers answered. It is interesting to observe that even the passing motorcyclists make the traditional *wai* of respect as they pass, temporarily abandoning their handlebars at full speed! For a good view of the shrine, climb onto the elevated pedestrian walkway crossing this busy junction.

Erawan Shrine
Opening times: 9am to 5pm daily
Admission: free

Note: Makrut
Thai chess, or *makrut*, is played everywhere in Bangkok, and at all times of the day and night. More like a simplified version of the Japanese game of Go than Western chess, it is often played on sheets of tattered cardboard with bottle caps for pieces.

Prathunam Market

With your back to the Erawan Shrine walk up Ratchadamri Road. **Central World** will be on your right occupying the entire city block and set well back from the street. This vast shopping complex also contains a convention centre and an office and a hotel tower all built between 2005 and 2007. Continue along Ratchadamri Road by crossing the bridge over Khlong San Sap and you will end up on Ratchaprarop Road. The **Prathunam Market** will be on your left. This popular market takes up most of this city block. Prathunam means 'water gate' in Thai and refers to the canal lock which used to be located on Khlong San Sap here. Also known as Chalermlok, this market occupies a maze of covered stalls and is a favourite place for Thais to shop, it is particularly good for cheap Indian fabrics as well as sewing accessories and also stocks a wide range of general domestic items. It is also a popular late-night eating spot, with noodle shops and food stalls staying open long after the nearby bars and cinemas have closed.

Prathunam Market
Opening times: 9am to midnight daily
Admission: free

Central World

Baiyoke Tower II

Continue along Ratchaprarop Road and take the first roadway to your left and you will be able to see the 309-metre-high Baiyoke Tower II ahead of you. Designed by Bangkok-based firm, Plan Architecture, the balconies on the nearby Baiyoke Tower I, designed by the same firm, have been painted a rainbow range of colours that seem to dissolve into one another as they ascend the building. When it was built the Baiyoke Tower I was the tallest structure in the city, it was quickly surpassed by any number of newer developments and now seems completely dwarfed by its newer neighbours. The Baiyoke Tower II is still the tallest building in Thailand. Perhaps the top of it could have been finished off a little more elegantly, it seems to be a poor imitation of New York's gorgeous 1920s skyscrapers, but it is still an impressive sight. The tower is home to a 400-room hotel and also contains an observation deck on

Prathunam

the 84th floor, which has breath-taking views of the city. It is best to wait for a haze-free day to get the clearest views. The access lift is glass and rapidly climbs one of the building's corners, which is fun in itself.

Baiyoke Tower II
Opening times: 10am to 10pm daily
Admission charges

Baiyoke Tower II

Link to the Wireless Road walk:
Walk back along Ratchaprarop Road, turn left onto New Petchburi Road and then right onto Wireless Road.

Wireless Road

Nearest Skytrain Station: Chidlom
Approximate walking time: 1 hour

Downtown East

Wireless Road and its surroundings is home to a number of embassies as well as some of the city's top hotels and interesting new skyscrapers. To the rear of the Swissotel is the charming little Nai Lert Shrine, while the road itself, known in Thai as Thanon Witthayu, was originally a narrow tree-lined track between two canals, sadly long since culverted. The area is also home to Lumphini Park, Bangkok's largest park and a delightful green lung in this overcrowded city.

THE WALK

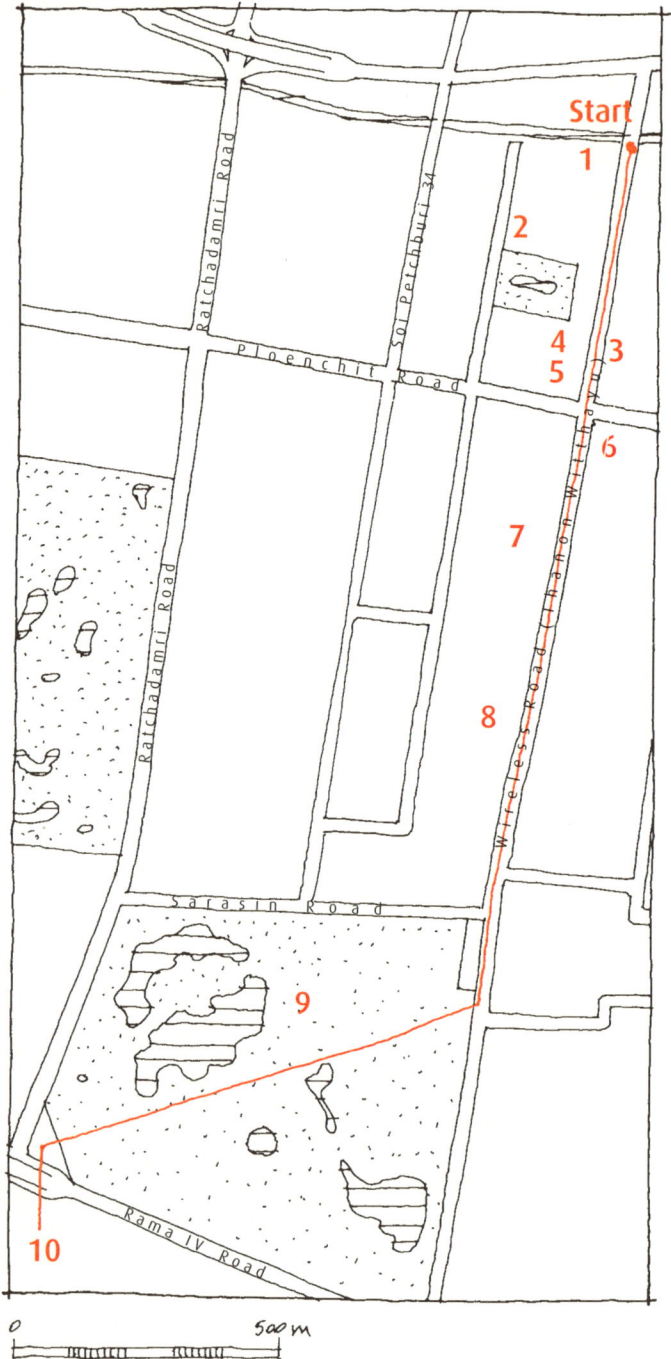

Start

1
2
3
4
5
6
7
8
9
10

Ratchadamri Road
Soi Petchburi 31
Ploenchit Road
Ratchadamri Road
Wireless Road (Thanon Witthayu)
Sarasin Road
Rama IV Road

0   500 m

KEY

1. Khlong San Sap

2. Nai Lert Park Shrine

3. Wireless Road

4. British Embassy

5. Central Embassy

6. Park Ventures Ecoplex

7. Royal Netherlands Embassy

8. US Embassy

9. Lumphini Park

10. Dusit Thani Hotel

Khlong San Sap

If you are walking from the Chidlom Skytrain Station, follow Ploenchit Road away from the direction of Ratchadamri Road, then turn left onto Wireless Road and you will come to the bridge over Khlong San Sap. This canal is an important arterial route and is one of only two major east-west canals that survive in Bangkok. It is a continuation of Khlong Mahanak and runs east through an area of marshland where Rama I banished the Muslim prisoners he captured during one of his southern campaigns — their descendants still live in an enclave on the north bank of the canal, roughly opposite Jim Thompson's house. The Prathunam district takes its name, which means 'water gate', from the canal lock that used to be located here.

Khlong San Sap

Note: Thai Royalty

The Chakri dynasty held absolute power for the first 150 years of its existence, and it still reigns today in the person of Rama IX. The first three kings tried to recreate their fallen capital of Ayutthaya in Bangkok, with Rama III's reign being marked by a strong Chinese influence. Rama IV, particularly after the signing of the Bowring Treaty (1855) and other similar agreements, ensured that Siam no longer looked inwards and to the past, but outwards, particularly towards the West, and his capital began to reflect this. Rama V's long reign, during a time of political difficulty in Southeast Asia, saw a continued expansion and a marked modernisation of the capital. The 20th century saw an explosion in Bangkok's growth, particularly the second half of the century which has blighted to a shameful extent what used to be a garden city crossed by numerous tree-lined canals.

Nai Lert Park Shrine

Continue along Wireless Road and you will come to the Swissotel. At the back of the hotel compound, opening onto a small winding *soi*, is the Nai Lert Shrine. Named after a Bangkok businessman who was famous in the first half of the twentieth century, the shrine is located on the edge of the lush grounds surrounding the elegant house he built for himself in 1905.

Dedicated to Chao Tuptim, a female animist spirit believed to reside in the old banyan tree here, this cluttered little shrine is famous for the hundreds of colourful stylised phalluses, mostly made of wood, which have been donated by grateful parents, invariably mothers, even though the faithful of both sexes pray here because the phallus is not just a fertility symbol, Thais also believe it can ensure prosperity. The shrine is located on the grounds of the Swissotel, originally built as the Hilton, a low-rise stepped building with an airy atrium facing onto its lushly landscaped grounds. It is home to a variety of excellent bars and restaurants.

Banyan tree shrine

Shrine, Nai Lert Park

BRACKEN DEC '09

BRACKEN JULY '01

Villa, Wireless Rd

Wireless Road

Return to Wireless Road and turn right. Still a relatively attractive and architecturally intact street, Thanon Witthayu, as it is called in Thai, is wide and well shaded by mature trees. Running from Petchburi Road in the north to the southeast corner of Lumphini Park, the road is home to a number of embassies, notably the American, British and Dutch, which still occupy

BRÜCKEN JUNE '09

spacious compounds. While some of the luxurious villas built by wealthy foreigners have been replaced by office towers and high-end hotels, there is still enough remaining to give a flavour of what this fashionable residential district must have looked like a century ago, a time when the parallel side lanes running along this road used to be *khlongs*.

MCM
XIV

1939

British Embassy

Follow Wireless Road to the junction with Ploenchit Road and the British Embassy compound will be on your right. A palatial collection of buildings, symmetrically laid out in an impressive enclosure on the corner of this busy junction, the compound could be mistaken for the residence of one of the minor members of the Thai royal family. The land was in fact purchased from wealthy businessman Nai Lert in the 1920s and its various buildings were designed in a gracious Neoclassical style well suited to the tropics. An elegant cenotaph commemorating the British dead in World Wars I and II sits as a focal point inside the main gates. The grounds are open to the public on the third Saturday of November each year for a hugely popular charity fair.

Did You Know?
Thailand's royal family has a strong American connection, the present king, Rama IX, was born in America, as was his brother, Rama VIII, while the King's eldest daughter was married to an American.

Central Embassy

Towering over the junction of Wireless and Ploenchit Roads is Central Embassy. Originally part of the British Embassy compound, this parcel of land was sold to the Central Group who developed their sinuous skyscraper hotel which slinks its way skywards over a seven-storey retail complex. An elegant design, it does its best not to overpower the elegant embassy buildings beneath. When the land was purchased in 2006 it broke the record for the most expensive in the kingdom (and was quite a windfall for the British government).

Central Embassy
Opening times: 10am to 10pm daily
Admission: free

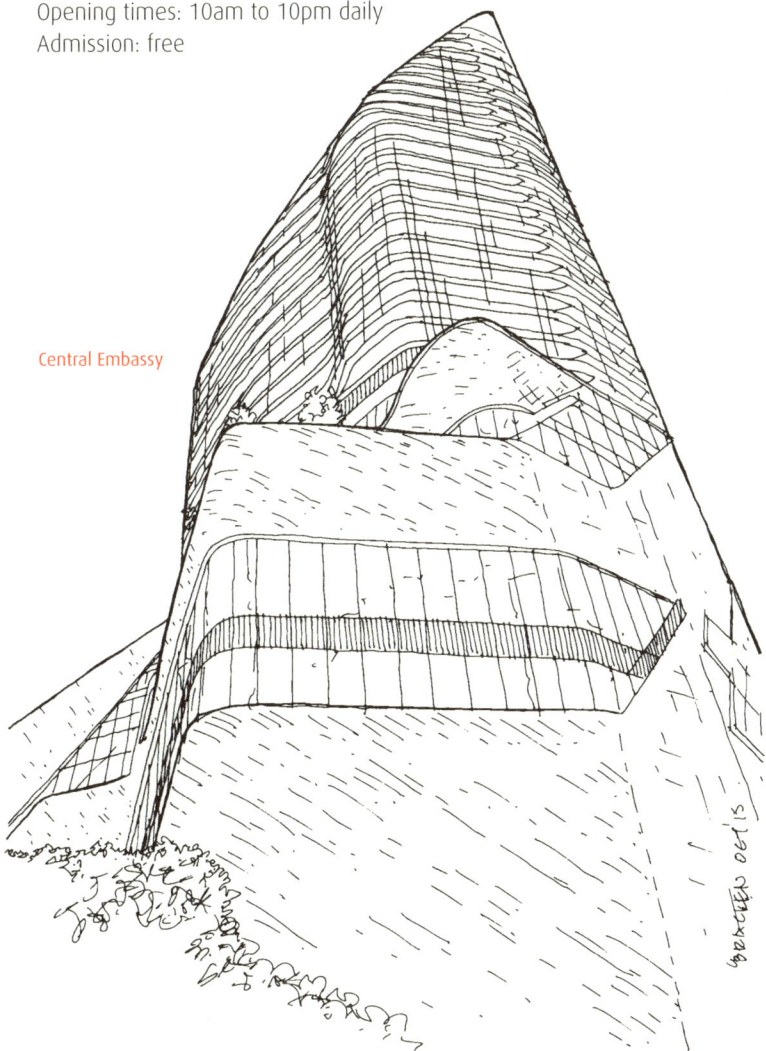

Central Embassy

Park Ventures Ecoplex

Diagonally across Wireless Road from Central Embassy towers another, altogether less elegant, skyscraper. Supposedly based on the unlikely combination of the traditional Thai greeting, the 'wai', and a lotus bud it was completed in 2011 and consists of offices and an hotel. The building features a series of eco-friendly devices, as its name suggests, and these include energy-saving glass (to reduce the need for air-conditioning) and a collection system for waste water so that it can be used for watering the landscaping.

Royal Netherlands Embassy

Continue down Wireless Road and you will see the gates and winding driveway of the Netherlands Embassy on your right. The embassy itself is a lovely white-painted wooden two-storey building with a tower that dates from the 1890s and sits in beautifully landscaped grounds. Originally built for a French doctor, the personal physician to Rama V, he moved out in 1913 and it was bought by a Thai prince. The Dutch government bought the house in 1948. It is one of the few surviving embassies in this part of the city — most having been sold off for profit and the houses knocked down to make way for tall new office towers.

US Embassy

Continue along Wireless Road and the US Embassy will be on your right, just after the US Ambassador's residential compound. The embassy is not a beautiful building. Like many American Embassies around the world, it looks more like a barracks. It is just a pity that it happens to be on such an attractive and relatively intact street. The **US Ambassador's Residence** is in stark contrast: pretty, small in scale, and consists of a number of unostentatious but comfortable-looking wooden villas dotted around a large, tree-shaded compound easily visible from the road. In harmony with the city, it is a throwback to what the district used to look like. Built for a British engineer around 1914, it was used as a home for Japanese troops during World War II. They left it in pretty bad condition. It became the US Ambassador's residence in 1946 and was beautifully restored (and again in the 1980s).

Lumphini Park

Continue along Wireless Road and you will come to Lumphini Park on your right. It's best to continue straight past the corner of the park, where there is a car park, and enter by the first gate on your right. This is a lovely large park right in the heart of Bangkok's downtown. Named after the Buddha's birthplace in Nepal, Lumphini Park was created by Rama VI as the site of a national exhibition, plans for which came to nothing after his death. There is

Lake, Lumphini Park

a statue commemorating him at the Silom Road corner. Considered vast when it was built, its edges have been somewhat eaten away by car parks and a number of ugly buildings but the park is still the largest single public green space in the city. It has two boating lakes, complete with islands, and some quaint bridges, as well as a number of pagodas and pavilions. The **Discovery Learning Centre** is an attractive mix of Western Neoclassicism with local Thai accents and was built as a library in the 1950s. The park also has an outdoor gym, which is extremely popular. The best time to visit is the early morning, when the park is at its busiest with joggers and hordes of pyjama-clad Chinese practising *tai chi chuan*.

Lumphini Park
Opening times: 4:30am to 9pm daily
Admission: free

Chinese Pavilion,
Lumphini Park

Wireless Road

Dusit Thani Hotel

Dusit Thani Hotel

Exit Lumphini Park via the main entrance, where the statue of Rama VI faces out over the busy junction of Ratchadamri and Rama IV Roads. There is an underpass under Rama IV Road which leads to the entrance of the Dusit Thani Hotel. A Bangkok institution since it was built in 1970, it was one of the tallest buildings in the city for over a decade. The triangular floor plan is intricate and clever and the subtle tapering of the tower has meant that it hasn't dated as badly as some of its less elegant contemporaries. Built on what was the compound of an important government official, the complex still feels spacious. Home to excellent bars and restaurants, it is an ideal place to stop and rest and maybe even have some refreshments.

Link to the Silom Road walk:
Leave the Dusit Thani Hotel compound by turning left onto Silom Road and then take the next left onto Sala Daeng Road.

Silom Road

Nearest Skytrain Station: Sala Daeng
Approximate walking time: 2 hours

Downtown South

The commercial heart of Bangkok, the Silom Road area is home to myriad offices, shops and restaurants. Towards the river end of the road, and also on parallel Suriwong Road, a number of shops specialise in gems, antiques and silk. The night market on Patpong Sois 1 and 2 draws huge crowds every night (except Wednesdays, when it's closed). The stretch of road between Patpong and Lumphini Park is home to some of the city's most popular bars and nightclubs, including a thriving gay scene. Silom Road also contains some surprises, such as the large Christian cemetery which has somehow miraculously survived.

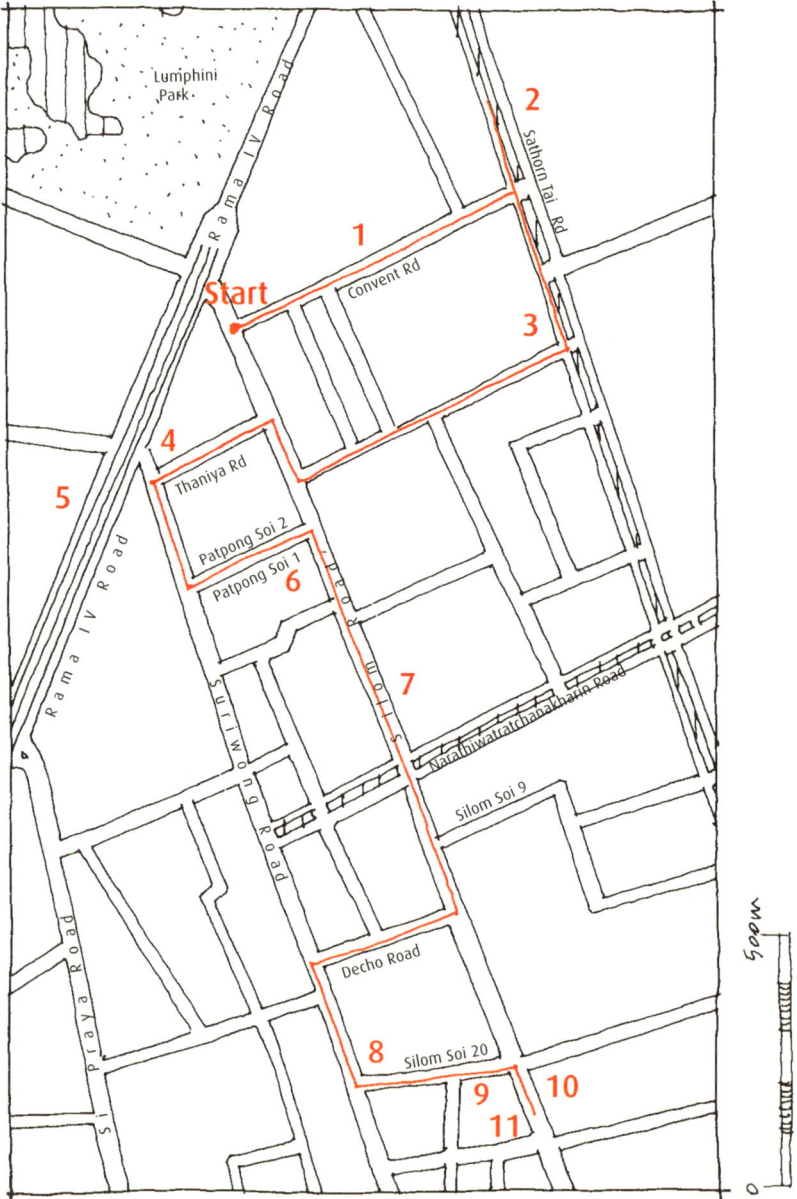

THE WALK

Lumphini Park

Rama IV Road

2

Sathorn Tai Rd

1

Start

Convent Rd

3

4

Thaniya Rd

5

Rama IV Road

Patpong Soi 2

6

Patpong Soi 1

Patpong Soi 1

Suriwong Road

7

Narathiwatratchanakharin Road

Silom Soi 9

Si Praya Road

Decho Road

8

Silom Soi 20

9

10

11

500m

0

KEY

1. Sala Daeng Road

2. Sathorn Road

3. Christ Church

4. Jim Thompson's Thai Silk Company

5. Snake Farm

6. Patpong Night Market

7. Silom Road

8. Neilson-Hays Library

9. Mirasuddeen Mosque

10. Sri Mahamariamman Temple

11. Silom Village

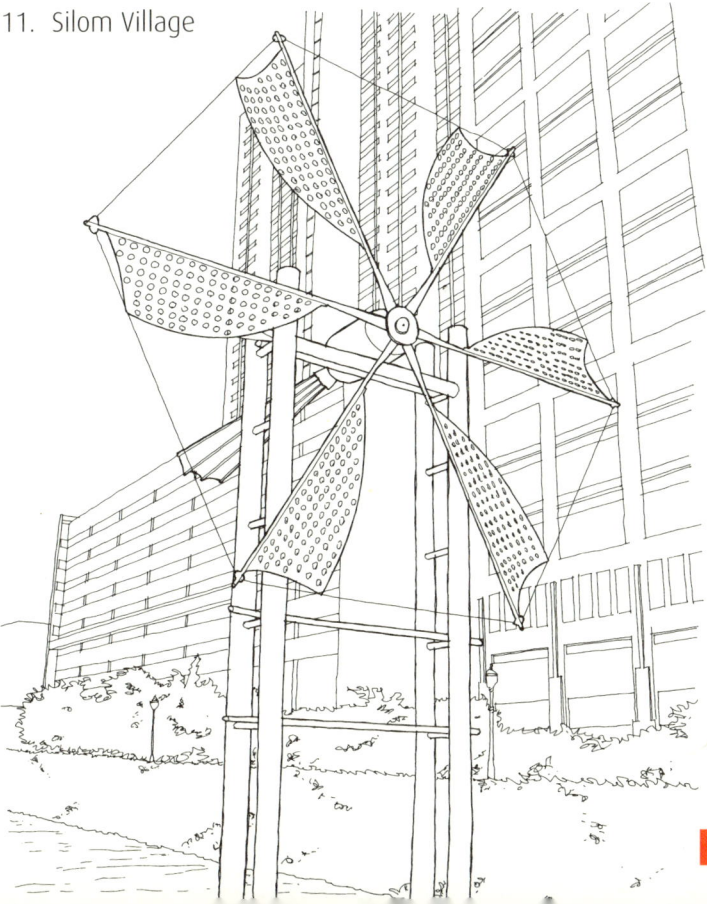

Silom Road

Sala Daeng Road

If you are walking from the Sala Daeng Skytrain Station, walk up Silom Road in the direction of Lumphini Park and turn right onto Sala Daeng Road. The corner here has some old shophouses, much in need of renovation but they give you an idea of what this part of the city used to look like before all the skyscrapers began to pop up.

Sathorn Road

Continue along Sala Daeng Road until you come to Sathorn Road and turn left. This was once an elegant, tree-lined boulevard but recent decades have seen it turned into a traffic-choked mess. At the beginning of the twentieth century this was the fashionable heart of expatriate life in Bangkok. Large villas sat in spacious tree-shaded grounds. Most of these have gone, replaced by hotels and office towers, but a few, like the Russian Embassy, remain and give a hint of what life must have been like for the privileged foreign residents of Bangkok a century ago.

The southern side of Sathorn Road has some of the city's most exclusive and beautiful hotels. Beginning with **the Sukhothai,** a large and luxurious hotel which has an understated elegance that manages to be both modern and distinctly Thai. The long, low buildings were built in 1991 and have shady colonnades overlooking beautiful pools and gardens, some of which feature traditional-looking chedis. The hotel's interior makes generous use of shimmering silk on its wall panels and has an impressive collection of contemporary terracotta bas reliefs replicating ones found in Sukhothai, Thailand's ancient capital. The hotel's Sunday brunch is a Bangkok institution.

The **Westin Banyan Tree Hotel**, back towards Sala Daeng Road, occupies the 33rd to the 60th floors of the taller of the two Thai Wah Towers. It has a spectacular open-air swimming pool located in the multi-storey opening punched high up through the fabric of the building and is a pleasant place to have a cocktail

Sukhothai Hotel

Silom Road

while watching the sun set over the city and see the lights of the neighbouring skyscrapers come on. This is also the best way to get a feel for this still attractive district, with its low-rise villas set in expansive grounds, as well as nearby Lumphini Park. The newest luxury hotel to open its doors in this select neighbourhood is the **Metropolitan**, a stylishly designed boutique hotel, part of the exclusive Como Group. Its smaller size makes it feel more intimate and, apart from the usual bars and restaurants, it is also home to some excellent artwork, some of it by local artists.

Thai Wah Towers 1 and 2

Christ Church

Continue along Sathorn Road and turn right at the junction with Convent Road. Before you do so, however, look to your left down Sathorn Road and you will see the towering apartment complex known as **The Met**. This elegant building is a cut above the usual residential complexes of Bangkok. Designed by WOHA architects, its 66 storeys show considerable engineering ingenuity as well as a

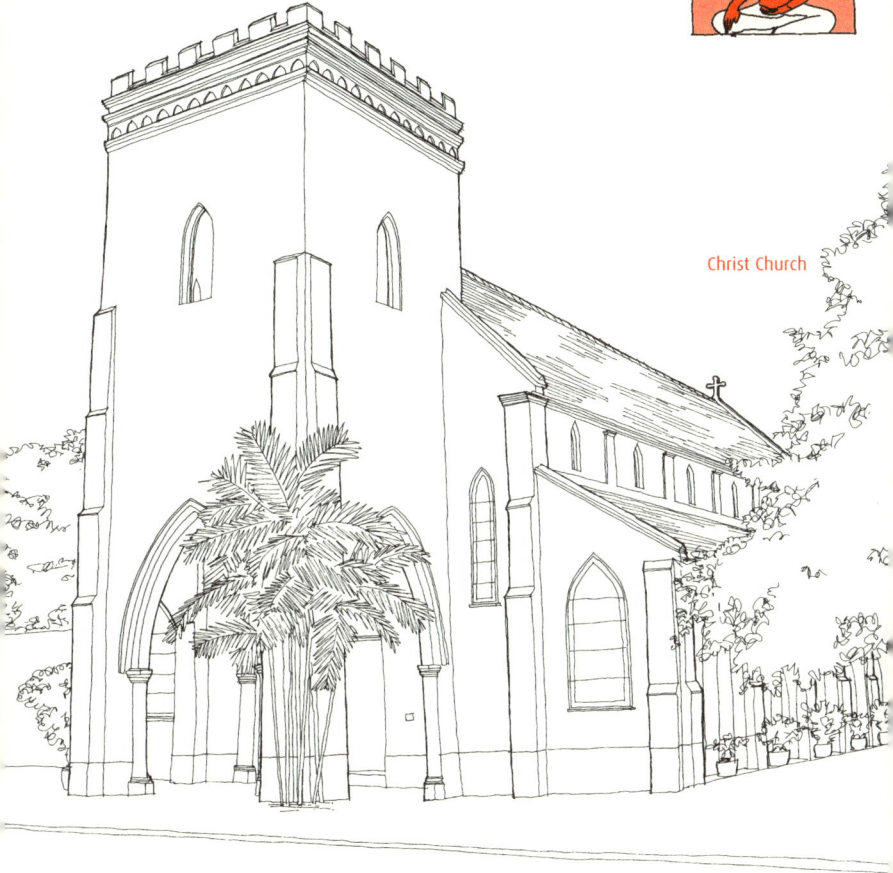

Christ Church

sensitivity to sustainability. At the corner where Convent Road meets Sathorn Road stands the delicate gothic-style **Christ Church**. This pretty little church looks rather like an Anglican parish church and seems, as a result, a little lost among the swaying palm trees. Actually it is ecumenical and was built in 1905 on land donated by Rama V for the large Christian community living in the area. Convent Road took its name from the Carmelite Convent and school that is still located halfway down its tree-lined length.

Did You Know?

The bell tower of Christ Church didn't originally have any bells for fear of disturbing a nearby nursing home but as the traffic grew increasingly louder bells were finally allowed in the 1950s.

Silom Road

Jim Thompson's Thai Silk Company

Follow Convent Road to the end and turn right onto Silom Road, then take the next left onto Thaniya Road. Follow it to the end and turn right onto Suriwong Road and you will see Jim Thompson's Thai Silk Company on your right. The flagship store of this exclusive chain, the handsome building was built in the style of seventeenth-century Ayutthaya and is a Suriwong Road landmark. It opened in 1967, just two weeks before Jim Thompson mysteriously disappeared in Malaysia, and the showrooms offer a tempting array of Thai silk in its many forms — from clothing and accessories, to bolts of raw fabric for use in tailoring or home furnishing. A coffee shop decorated in the style of Jim Thompson's House is located on the second floor.

Jim Thompson's Thai Silk Company
Opening times: 9am to 9pm daily
Admission: free

Jim Thompson's Thai Silk Company

Snake Farm

Turn right after you leave the Jim Thompson's Thai Silk Company and you will see, across Rama IV Road in front of you, on the left-hand side of Henri Dunant Road, the Queen Saovapha Snake Farm. Originally called the Pasteur Institute, it was renamed in honour of the wife of Rama V. Run by the Thai Red Cross, it is home to a better collection of snakes than even Dusit Zoo, while its emphasis, unlike other Thai snake farms, is on education, with a slide show before its twice daily demonstrations of venom milking (which takes place only once on weekends). The snake venom is used in the production of anti-snake-bite serum.

Across Henri Dunant Road is **Chulalongkorn Hospital**, a series of fine European-style neoclassical buildings with some of their elements, like the overhanging eaves, adapted to suit the tropical climate. These are generally in quite good condition, but as the busy hospital has had to expand and improve itself over the years, some of the earlier buildings have been insensitively added to, with the result that these architectural gems, especially the one whose side faces onto Lumphini Park, can hardly be seen anymore.

Snake Farm

Opening times: 9:30am to 3:30pm, Mon-Fri; 9:30 to 1pm, Sat-Sun
Admission charges

Chulalongkorn Hospital

BRACKEN MAY '01

Silom Road

Patpong Night Market

Continue along Suriwong Road until you come to Patpong Soi 2 on your left. Patpong Sois 1 and 2 take their name from their original owner and developer, a Chinese businessman called Patpongpanit. They are still privately owned and have become one of the city's most popular night markets (as well as one of the world's most notorious red-light districts). Patpong is best known for its fake brands — everything from clothes to watches and DVDs — and is slowly colonising the neighbouring stretches of Silom Road. This area first became popular in the 1960s, when American soldiers on leave from active service in the Vietnam War used to visit for rest and recreation. In the 1990s, more fashionable bars and nightclubs began to carve a niche for themselves among the sleazy go-go bars and massage parlours, even though these still are still thriving. Silom Sois 4 and 2 have a lively gay scene, which is quite open and generally very mixed, while Thaniya Road is almost exclusively Japanese, to the extent that other nationalities are even barred from entering some of the entertainment establishments.

Patpong Night Market
Opening times: 9pm to 2am daily, except Wed
Admission: free

Silom Road

Wander the lanes and alleyways of Patpong and when you're ready to leave turn right onto Silom Road. This is a relatively narrow street lined by increasingly tall buildings. The northern part of it is further darkened by the Sala Daeng Skytrain Station. Home to fashionable offices, shops and restaurants, it's hard to believe that just a generation or two ago this was a canal with orchards on either side. A faint reminder of those days is the sight of thousands of barn swallows that come to nest in the few remaining trees between October and March.

Walking along Silom Road, away from the Sala Daeng Skytrain Station, and you will come to the whimsical little windmill sculpture sitting at the heart of the busy junction of roadway and water where Silom Road crosses the canal at Narathiwatratchanakharin Road. This sculpture takes its name from Silom Road — Silom being Thai for windmill. Located on either side of Silom Soi 9 (Soi Suksa Witthaya), which is the next left after Narathiwatratchanakharin Road, are **Christian cemeteries**. Run-down but charming, these used to be the property of the Assumption Cathedral, which is located not too far away, just off Soi Oriental (Charoen Krung Soi 40). Active since the 1950s, new zoning laws in the 1990s forbade burying the dead in central Bangkok, which also means that all existing remains will have to be moved elsewhere eventually. Some of the cemeteries' monuments are quite impressive, particularly the

Windmill

Xavier Crypt, which consists of a large white octagon sitting at the heart of the second graveyard and directly in line with the pitched-roofed wooden gateway.

Farther along Silom Road, just past the Christian cemeteries, there is a small **Chinese cemetery** with an elegantly decorative gateway.

Did You Know?
Silom means 'windmill' in Thai, and this roadway derives its name from the water pumps that used to be located in the area.

Neilson-Hays Library

Turn right off Silom Road onto Decho Road and follow it to the end. Then turn left onto Suriwong Road and the **British Club** will be on your left at number 189. Founded in 1903 as an all-male (and all-white) businessman's club (now with a more inclusive approach to membership) it is housed in an elegant two-storey white Georgian-style mansion built in 1910 that would not look out of place in the rolling English countryside.

Next door to it is the **Neilson-Hays Library**, located on the corner of Suriwong Road and Soi Pradit (also known as Silom Soi 20). Housed in an elegant neoclassical building which dates from 1921, the library began as a small reading group consisting of the wives of missionaries but grew into the impressive collection of 20,000 volumes that is housed here today — one of the most important English-language libraries in Southeast Asia. This single-storey, symmetrical building was named in honour of Jennie Neilson-Hays, a mainstay of the Bangkok Library Association from 1895 to 1920, and was paid for by her husband, Dr Hays. The library's elegant curved entrance leads into a small domed rotunda which now acts as a small modern-art gallery. It also has a charming H-shaped reading room.

Neilson-Hays Library
Opening times: 9:30am to 4pm, Tue–Sun
Admission: free

Neilson-Hays Library

52

Mirasuddeen Mosque

Turn left onto Soi Pradit (Silom Soi 20) and halfway along you will see the Mirasuddeen Mosque on your right. Thailand has a significant minority population of Muslims, mostly from the south, particularly Pattani, which until the beginning of the 20th century was an independent sultanate owing tribute to Siam. Originally a wooden structure built around 1912, this temple was built in the 1990s by an Indian who dedicated himself to Bangkok's Muslims. It faces a Muslim charity organisation which helps the poor, educates children and even collects unclaimed bodies in the city. Next door to the mosque is **Talad Soi Prachum**, a colourful wet market housed in a 1930s-style concrete shed actually built in the late 1960s.

Mirasuddeen Mosque
Opening times: 5am to 8pm daily
Admission: free

Mirasuddeen Mosque

Sri Mahamariamman Temple

At the end of Soi Pradit (Silom Soi 20), turn right onto Silom Road and you will see on your left the Sri Mahamariamman Temple, which is also known as the Maha Uma Devi Temple. After 1858, when India became a British Crown Colony, a number of southern Indians and Ceylonese (Sri Lankans) decided to move to Bangkok rather than stay in their own country under British rule. Many of them were Tamils and a group of them founded this colourful Hindu temple during the following decade. The main building of the complex has a gold-plated copper dome behind a six-metre-high gopuram featuring various Hindu gods. The style is traditional Dravidian. The Thai name for the temple is Wat Khaek (or Guests' Temple) but an underlying cross cultural heritage means that many Thais and Chinese actually worship here — the Hindu

deities Shiva and Ganesh are revered by Thai Buddhists, while Hindus regard the Buddha as one of the incarnations of Vishnu. Although always busy, the temple is particularly worth visiting around November when it is lit up for Deepavali (the Festival of Light), the Indian New Year. During the rest of the year an oil lamp ritual is held most middays and on Fridays at 11:30am there is a *prasada* (vegetarian ceremony), in which blessed food is distributed to devotees.

Sri Mahamariamman Temple
Opening times: 6am to 8pm daily
Admission: free

Note: Deepavali
Indian temples and homes are decorated with lights to mark the Indian New Year which is calculated annually according to Indian almanacs; sometimes occurring in October but more often in November. Also known as the Festival of Light, this is when Hindus mark Lord Krishna's victory over Narakasura, which is seen as a triumph of good over evil, symbolised by light overcoming darkness.

Silom Village
Almost opposite Sri Mahamariamman Temple on Silom Road is Silom Village, an attractive reuse of 17 old houses that opened in 1980 and has become a thriving centre for traditional Thai handicrafts. The houses themselves hark back to a time when Silom Road was a pleasant residential district popular with Westerners. The complex also contains a number of Thai restaurants as well as a small hotel.

BRACKEN JULY '01

Jewelry Trade Centre

Jewelry Trade Centre

Continue along Silom Road and you will come to the Jewelry Trade Centre on your left. This slender 59-storey tower, with a vaguely Art Deco feel is home to the country's largest jewelry sorting and distribution centre. Built in 1996, it was the tallest building in the city at the time (currently it is the eighth tallest). The tower's lower floors are home to **Silom Galleria**, which contains a number of shops dedicated to art, antiques and of course jewelry.

Silom Galleria
Opening times: 10am to 10pm daily
Admission: free

Link to the Charoen Krung Road walk:
Follow Silom Road to the end, turn left onto Charoen Krung Road and the Bangrak Market will be on your right between Charoen Krung Sois 44 and 46.

Charoen Krung Road

Nearest Skytrain Station: Saphan Taksin
Approximate walking time: 1 hour 30 minutes

Old European Quarter

This was originally the location of Bangkok's port and saw much foreign commercial activity throughout the nineteenth century, which in turn resulted in a number of elegant, Western-style buildings, starting with the Portuguese Chancellery, built on land granted in 1820, and the French Embassy, built shortly afterwards. Other buildings soon followed in answer to Westerners' increasing needs. The area is also home to some charming temples and a mosque as well as thriving markets, including a stamp market at the old General Post Office, and Bangkrak Market, where this walk begins.

THE WALK

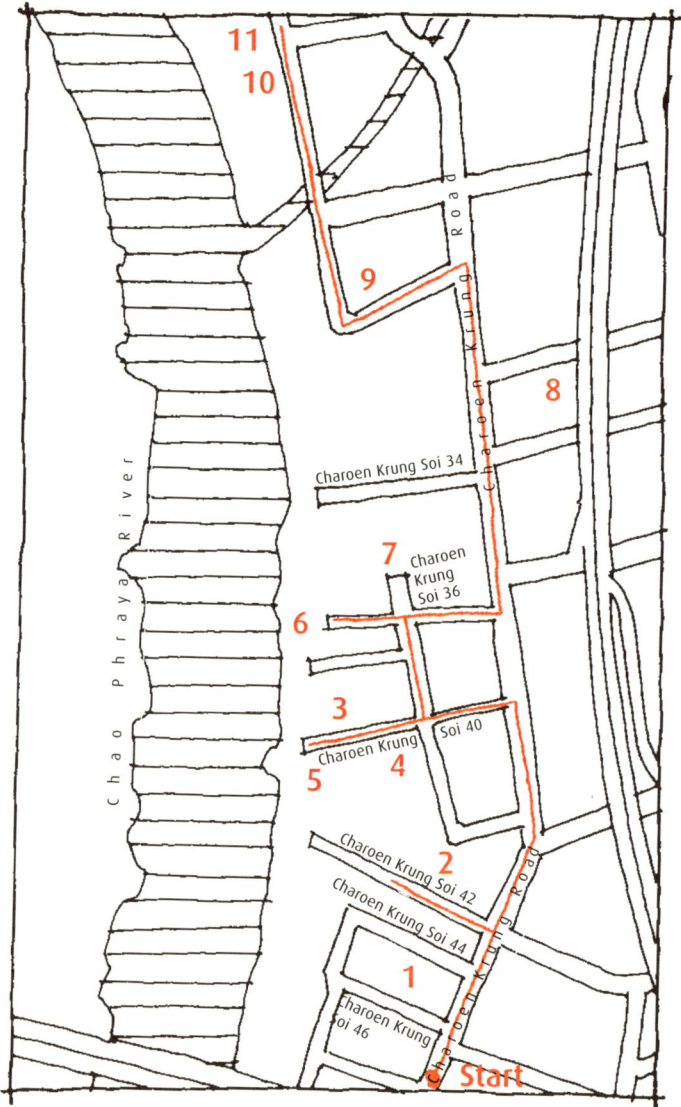

11
10
9
8

Charoen Krung Soi 34

7 Charoen
Krung
Soi 36

6

3
4 Soi 40

5 Charoen Krung

Charoen Krung Soi 42 2

Charoen Krung Soi 44

1

Charoen Krung
Soi 46

Start

Chao Phraya River

Charoen Krung Road

0   500m

KEY

1. Bangrak Market
2. Wat Suan Phu
3. Oriental Hotel
4. Assumption Cathedral
5. East Asiatic Company
6. Old Customs House
7. Haroon Mosque
8. Bangkok Folk Museum
9. Captain Bush House
10. Holy Rosary Church
11. Siam Commercial Bank

Charoen Krung Road

Bangrak Market

If you are coming from the Saphan Taksin Skytrain Station turn left onto Charoen Krung Road and the Bangrak Market will be on your left between Charoen Krung Sois 44 and 46. This small but busy market is open every day and supplies many of the nearby hotels with fruit, vegetables, meat and seafood. It also has a fabric and clothes section.

Wat Suan Phu

Wander the sois between Charoen Krung Road and the river at will. In the reign of Rama V, sections of the old city wall were demolished to provide foundations for roads, this being the first of them. Loathe to see all traces of the city walls vanish, Rama V preserved two of the original 14 fortified towers; Mahakath Fort near the Golden Mount, and Phra Sumen Fort on Phra Athit Road are still standing today.

Running through the heart of Bangkok's old European community, from Yannawa in the south, all the way through Chinatown to Wat Pho in the north, Charoen Krung, or New Road, was Thailand's first paved highway and linked the Customs House to the many trading companies in the area. It is home to many gem and antique traders. A tram line started in 1892 also used to run along the road but the last tram vanished from the city in 1965. While

Shophouse,
Charoen Krung Road

Wat Suan Phu

the road itself is choked with traffic, pollution and noise, the side streets, particularly the ones leading to the river, are lined with trees and some really lovely wooden houses and seem quiet as country lanes.

Between Charoen Krung Road and the river runs the narrow Charoen Krung Soi 42. Approached by the decorative arch on Charoen Krung Road, **Wat Suan Phu** is on the right-hand side of this little laneway. A simple wooden temple with some finely carved detailing, it dates from 1797 and was founded by Chinese merchants. The Ordination Hall was built in 1798, but the Gathering Hall not until the 1930s. Well known for its Phra Bodhisattvakuan-In, a Chinese shrine positioned over the carp pond, most of the compound's buildings have been sensitively restored and are painted prettily.

Oriental Hotel

When you have finished wandering the sois near the river, return to Charoen Krung Road and turn left. Follow the road until you come to Soi Oriental (Charoen Krung Soi 40), which will be on your left. Near the end of this *soi* you will see the Oriental Hotel on you right. One of the world's most celebrated hotels, it was established in the 1880s by a Danish sea captain before being sold to the Armenian Sarkies brothers (who also founded the E&O in Penang and Raffles Hotel in Singapore). There had been hotels here before, the first being a seaman's hostel run by an American sea captain which burnt down in the 1860s. The second was the property of another captain, a Dane, who sold it on to fellow countryman, also a captain, and it was he who had the current iconic building built. Designed in a lightly handled Venetian style by a

Charoen Krung Road

Bangkok-based Italian architect, two wings were added in the 20th century: the Tower Wing in 1958 and the River Wing in 1976, neither of which add greatly to the hotel's charm (although they don't overly disturb it, and they do make it more comfortable). Repeatedly voted the world's best hotel, the original white-shuttered building still overlooks a small but lavishly planted garden. This is the wing that contains the Authors' Suites. There is also an Authors' Lounge, where afternoon tea is served and concerts sometimes performed.

Overlooking the entrance to the hotel is **China House**. Located in a pretty building dating from the 1920s, its delicate fretwork makes it look almost edible, which is appropriate since it is home to one of Bangkok's most expensive restaurants. Originally built as a home, it was for a while a consulate and is now part of the Oriental Hotel. The neighbouring building, the Commercial Company of Siam, was erected at around the same time and also features beautifully decorative woodwork.

Note: Writers

Joseph Conrad, in his novel *The Shadow Line*, wrote about journeying up the Chao Phraya River, W. Somerset Maugham described his impressions of Thailand in the 1920s in *The Gentleman in the Parlour*, while more recently, Alex Garland gave a brief but devastating description of life on Khao San Road for backpackers in search of the perfect getaway in *The Beach*. No list of Westerners writing about Bangkok would be complete, however, without Anna Leonowens, the English governess at Rama IV's court whose memoirs were the basis for the musical *The King and I* (which is actually banned in Thailand for the inaccuracies of its portrayal of a much revered king). Conrad and Maugham have had suites at the Oriental Hotel named after them, while some of the other authors so honoured make for rather a mixed bag, they include Noel Coward, Gore Vidal, Graham Greene, James Michener and Barbara Cartland — writers who seem to have simply stayed at the hotel rather than have added anything to Thailand's canon. Perhaps they should honour some of their own? S.P. Somtow is an excellent Thai writer, his *Jasmine Nights* a delightful read, or Kukrit Pramoj, who wrote the magnificent *Four Reigns*.

Assumption Cathedral

Across the *soi* from the Oriental Hotel is a wide passageway under a delightful Venetian-style arch which leads to a small pedestrian square overlooked by Assumption Cathedral. This very French-looking brick-and-stucco building dates from 1910 and was built on the site of an earlier cathedral founded almost a century earlier. Twin towers flank a somewhat plain romanesque façade. The interior is a startling contrast with a high barrel vault with square panels of blue-painted infill sporting golden stars (the symbol of Our Lady of the Assumption). Delicately lit by a large rose window, the interior was damaged during World War II but was painstakingly restored. The rather imposing

Arch, East Asiatic Company

altar is marble and comes from France. The little square that the cathedral faces onto is one of a kind in the city — no cars are allowed onto it, and its scale and general atmosphere is quite French, it's a pity more isn't done with it. The square is also overlooked by the **Assumption Press** (originally the Roman Catholic Mission Press) established over the river in Thonburi in 1795 by a priest who brought a printing press with him all the way from France. This simple yet noble neoclassical building contains a deep loggia over its entrance and is handsomely detailed with Roman Doric columns.

Assumption Cathedral

Charoen Krung Road

Catholic Mission

East Asiatic Company

East Asiatic Company

When you've finished wandering around this delightful little enclave, retrace your steps under the arch, turn left and continue down Soi Oriental (Charoen Krung Soi 40), following it to the end where it overlooks the river. On your left you will see the East Asiatic Company, founded in the 1880s by the same Danish captain who established the nearby Oriental Hotel. This is still one of the world's main trading conglomerates, although it moved from here in the 1990s. Registered as a national monument in 2001, this lively Venetian-style building was built around 1900. The plasterwork is very good, particularly the decorative panels over the windows that feature the caduceus.

Old Customs House

Retrace your steps back along Soi Oriental and take the first left after the Oriental Hotel. **O.P. Place** will be on your right after Charoen Krung Soi 38. Originally an import and wholesale business, it was one of the largest foreign-owned buildings in the country when built in 1908. This is the second building on this site and is in an assured neoclassical idiom. It was sensitively converted into an upmarket shopping centre specialising in Asian arts and antiques in the 1980s. Continue along the *soi*, keeping O.P. Place on your right, and you will come to the **French Embassy** on your left at the corner of Charoen Krung Soi 36.

For the first century or so of Bangkok's history all foreign legations were located on or near the Chao Phraya River as the river was the easiest way for representatives to get to and from the Grand Palace on official business. The French have had a long history of diplomatic relations with Thailand, having had an embassy at Ayutthaya in the 17th century, while Siam established an embassy at the court of Louis XIV in Versailles. The French Embassy is the second oldest in the city (the Portuguese being slightly older). It was built in the middle of the 19th century but has been gradually added to over the years. The ambassador's residence has some fine timber fretwork and overlooks a lawn that leads down to the river. A broad veranda runs along the living quarters on the upper floor, this was a common feature of buildings at the time because it was effective for shading, air circulation, and acted as a protection from flooding.

With the French Embassy on your left follow Charoen Krung Soi 36 to the end where, on your left overlooking the river, you will see the **Old Customs House.** This badly-neglected but still majestic neoclassical building is one of the finest remaining European-style structures in the city. Built in the 1880s, it was once the Thai Customs Department, and is now home to a fire brigade. The Treasury Department has registered the building with the Fine Arts Department as an historic site and private investors are in discussion to renovate it and convert it into a Thai cultural centre.

French Embassy

Haroon Mosque

Retrace your steps back along Charoen Krung Soi 36, past the French Embassy on your right, and cross the small junction of *sois* in front of it and you will see the Haroon Mosque on your left. This tiny mosque is aligned towards Mecca and sits at the heart of a small Muslim enclave. Behind it there is also a small Muslim graveyard. Most of the surrounding houses are wooden, and many are quite beautifully detailed, with delicately carved fretwork on fascias and grilles. Most are crammed together and leave their doors open offering glimpses into the inhabitants' way of life. Some of them are quite large and handsome, sitting within their own compounds and surrounded by lush tropical greenery.

Across the *soi* from the mosque is a small but delightful public garden, full of shady walkways and wooden benches where elderly residents sit in the shade and chat. Overlooking the other side of the garden you can see **Wat Muang Kae**, a lovely wooden Buddhist temple. To get to the *wat*, follow Charoen Krung Soi 36 to the end and turn left onto Charoen Krung Road. Take the next left onto Charoen Krung Soi 34 and follow it to the end, past a large school. Wat Muang Kae will be at the end of the *soi* on your left.

Haroon Mosque

House, Charoen Krung Soi 36

Bangkok Folk Museum

Retrace your steps along Charoen Krung Soi 34 and turn left onto Charoen Krung Road and the rather imposing looking **General Post Office** will be on your left. Set well back from the road, this large, rather squat-looking building dates from 1940, which may explain its vaguely fascist air. This is a rather heavy-handed version of the Art Deco style. The top corners of the central block are decorated with *garudas* (mythical half-bird-half-human creatures) and there is a statue of Rama V in front. The wide forecourt was revamped in 2013 and is home to a popular Stamp Market every Sunday (Thailand's stamps are avidly collected); the market also sells coins.

Just after the post office on the right is Charoen Krung Soi 43, and nestling almost under the elevated expressway is a leafy compound consisting of a cluster of teak houses that is home to the **Bangkok Folk Museum**. Established in 1992, the Western-style main house dates from the 1930s and contains artefacts from that era giving a glimpse into life in Bangkok for the middle classes in the middle of the 20th century. The upper floor contains a Bankrak history gallery.

Bangkok Folk Museum
Opening times: 8:30am to 4pm, Mon–Thur
Admission: free

Charoen Krung Road

Captain Bush House

Retrace your steps down Charoen Krung Soi 43 and turn right onto Charoen Krung Road, then left onto Charoen Krung Soi 30. Just at the point where this *soi* veers sharply to the right you will see the **Portuguese Chancellery** on your left. The Portuguese were the first Europeans to trade with Siam, which they did from their base at Malacca in Malaysia since the early 16th century. Rama II granted this plot of land to their first consul in 1820, where they erected a factory, as trading stations were then known, which is now home to the embassy offices. The architectural development of the building is not known for certain, but the original consular residence would have been a simple structure, it was replaced around 1860 when better building materials became available. The present villa has a simple yet attractive neoclassical symmetrical façade that faces over the river, as most buildings did in those days, with upper rooms opening onto a wide veranda over the thick-walled lower floor.

Continue along Charoen Krung Soi 30, passing the **Royal Orchid Sheraton**, which will be on your left. **Captain Bush House** will be on your right. A charming symmetrical two-storey neoclassical house built for Captain Bush in 1890. Later promoted to admiral, Bush was a British sea captain who came to Thailand in the 1850s and ended up advising the government on naval matters. This pretty little house is currently being restored.

Captain Bush House

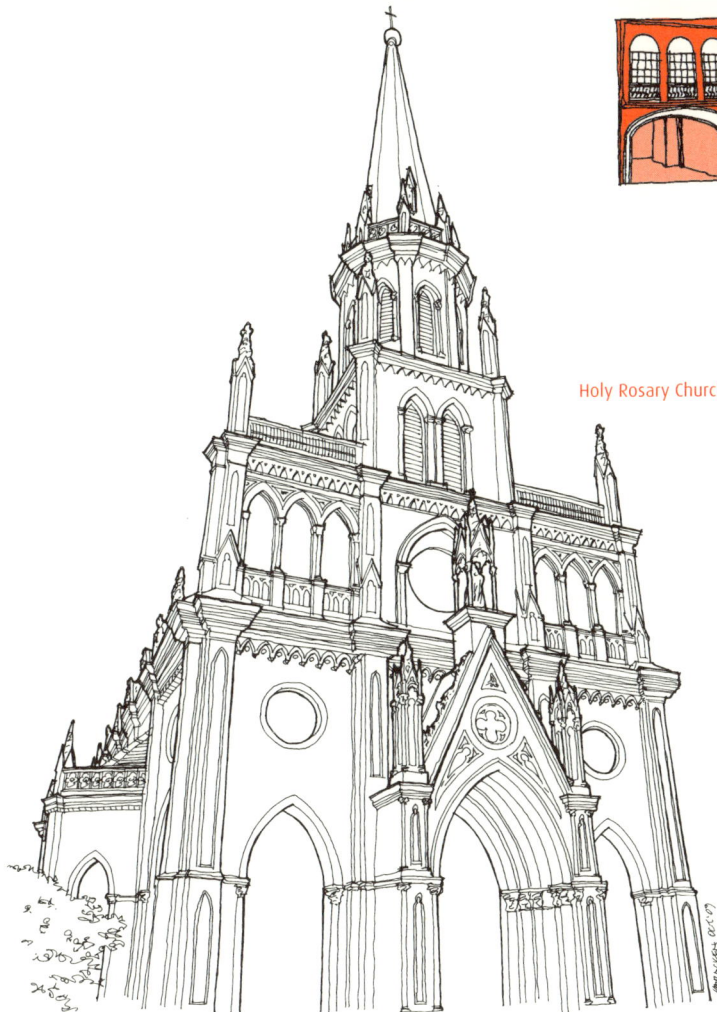

Holy Rosary Church

Holy Rosary Church

Continue along Charoen Krung Soi 30 which turns into Charoen Krung Soi 24 where it crosses **Khlong Padung Krung Kasem**. This quiet canal is one of the longest in the city, being the outermost of the three concentric rings dug by Rama I for the defence of the city. Like its sister canal, Khlong Bang Lamphoo, this is not so well preserved (Khlong Lord is the best of the three). Overlooking the canal on your left is the **River City Shopping Complex**, built in 1984 and revamped about 15 years later. It contains some nice cafes facing out over the river. Continue up Charoen Krung Soi 24, which leads you onto Soi Wanit 2, and you will come to the **Holy Rosary Church** on your left at the junction with Thanon Yotha. Also known as the Kalawar Church, it was founded by Portuguese Catholics who moved here after the sack of Ayutthaya. Rama I first granted the land here in 1786 to build a church and they named it using the Portuguese word for Calvary (the hill where Christ was crucified). This is the third church to stand on the site and is in a lovely light gothic style.

Siam Commercial Bank

Siam Commercial Bank

Continue along Soi Wanit 2 and almost immediately you will come to the gates that lead into the Siam Commercial Bank compound. This elegant, two-storey neoclassical building dates from 1908 and has been well taken care of, even winning a conservation award in the 1980s. It was renovated again in the mid-1990s and sits on a generous compound with some lovely mature planting commanding fine views of the river.

The Siam Commercial Bank was founded in 1906 on the advice of a Thai prince who had seen the advantages of modern banking. The building has two storeys over a basement and its facades are symmetrical. The one facing the river is particularly fine. It was designed by an Italian architect called Rogotti in a lightly handled Beaux Arts neoclassicism stylde and has been painted in subtly complementary colours.

Link to the Chinatown walk:

*Continue along Soi Wanit 2, which twists and turns through an old residential district of almost decrepit-looking wooden houses nestling amid overgrown greenery, until you come to the T-junction with Phanu Rangsi Alley and turn right. This alley skirts the leafy temple complex of **Wat Pathum Khonkha** and emerges onto Khao Lam Road, where you should turn left. Take the next right turn, a sharp angle onto Trimit Road, and you will see a Chinese gateway ahead of you.*

Chinatown

Nearest Chao Phraya Express Pier: Harbour Department
Approximate walking time: 1 hour and 30 minutes

Sampeng

One of Bangkok's most colourful and vibrant districts, Chinatown, or Sampeng as it is sometimes still known, is full of narrow sois teeming with activity, markets with colourful awnings to protect from the sun and rain, food stalls selling an amazing variety of snacks — not all palatable to Western tastes — and of course shophouses where raditional Chinese crafts continue to be practiced.

THE WALK

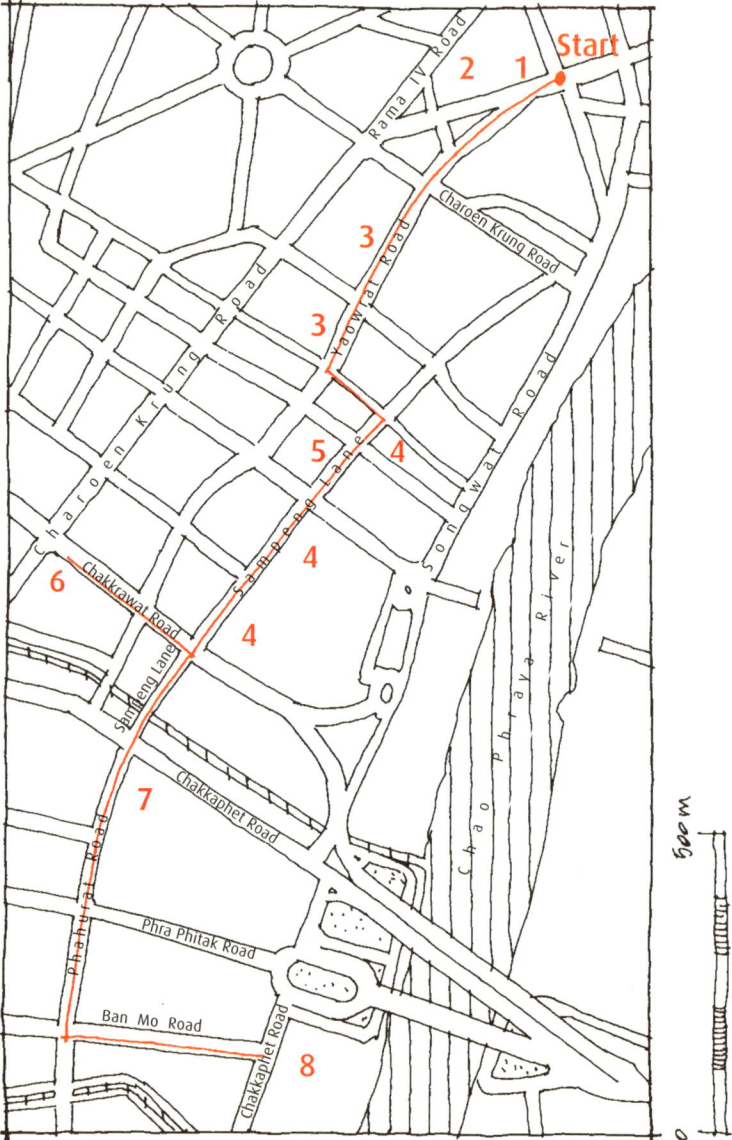

KEY

1. Yaowarat Chinatown Heritage Centre
2. Wat Trimit
3. Yaowarat Road
4. Sampeng Lane Market
5. Tang To Kang Gold Shop
6. Nakorn Kasem Market
7. Phahurat Market
8. Flower Market

Yaowarat Chinatown Heritage Centre

If you are coming from the Marine Department Chao Phraya Express Pier walk to Soi Wanit 2 and turn left. This narrow roadway twists and turns through an old residential district of wooden houses in overgrown gardens. When you come to the T-junction with Phanu Rangsi Alley turn right, skirting the temple complex of **Wat Pathum Khonkha** on your left, take the next left onto Khao Lam Road. Then take a right onto Trimit Road, which is at a sharp angle, and you will see a large Chinese-style gate ahead of you on a roundabout known as Odeon Circle, after a cinema (now demolished). This is where Trimit Road crosses Charoen Krung Road and a number of other streets converge.

The attractive and colourful gateway, known as **Chinatown Gate** (and also the King's Birthday Celebration Arch) was erected in 1999 and acts as an entry into Chinatown. Go around the roundabout and walk up Trimit Road and you will come to the **Yaowarat Chinatown Heritage Centre** on your left. Located in one of the old buildings when the neighbouring Wat Trimit got a makeover in 2009, this small museum gives a flavour of what life was like in Chinatown in the past via photos, prints and a number of tableaux, including scenes from shops on nearby Sampeng Lane.

Yaowarat Chinatown Heritage Centre
Opening times:
8am to 4:30pm daily
Admission charges

Pagoda from across the river at Chinatown

Wat Trimit

Wat Trimit

Located just behind the Yaowarat Chinatown Heritage Centre is the large and impressive complex of Wat Trimit. Also known as the Temple of the Golden Buddha, this Buddhist place of worship is best known for housing the world's largest solid gold statue of the Buddha. Although the temple's interior is also splendid, the highlight of any visit has to be the famous 18-carat gold statue, over three metres in height and weighing five-and-a-half tons. It was brought to Bangkok from Ayutthaya by Rama I and moved here in the 1930s. When it was being moved to a different part of the compound in the 1955 it was dropped and some of the plaster cracked off, revealing gold. Said to come from Sukhothai, this 13th-century statue was thought to have been encased in stucco to hide it from Burmese raiders, a common practice during the Ayutthaya period (the Emerald Buddha was also hidden in such a manner, although during a much earlier period, it too was only discovered to be of great value when some of its plaster accidently flaked off). Local Chinese residents come here to worship and make merit by rubbing gold leaf onto some of the temple's smaller Buddha images.

Wat Trimit
Opening times: 8am to 5pm daily
Admission charges

Chinatown

Art Deco corner building, Yaowarat Road

Yaowarat Road

Leave the temple and return to the Chinatown Gate and turn right up Yaowarat Road. This is Chinatown at its most atmospheric, with garish colours, pungent smells and overwhelming noise. This roadway is the main route through the heart of the district and is lined with gold shops, herb sellers, noodle stalls and a variety of restaurants, all under huge neon signs where the numerous Chinese characters crowd out the few Thai and English words that can be seen. It looks more like a street in Shanghai or Beijing than Bangkok and contains some fine if dilapidated old buildings, particularly a number of fine Art Deco corner buildings.

Note: The Chinese

Chinese merchants came to Thailand from the 14th century onwards. During the late-18th and early-19th centuries, following years of war in the country, Chinese immigration was actively encouraged in order to help rebuild the economy. The Chinese went on to integrate into Thai society so successfully that by the middle of the 19th century, half of Bangkok's population could claim to have at least some Chinese blood. Today, the Chinese continue to dominate Thailand's financial and commercial sectors.

Yaowarat Road

Did You Know?

Bangkok's Chinese residents originally lived in Rattanakosin, where the Grand Palace is now, but when Rama I decided to move his capital from across the river in Thonburi in 1782 the entire community was forced to relocate here.

Chinatown

Sampeng Lane Market

Continue along Yaowarat Road until you come to Soi Isara Nuphap and turn left. There are some interesting shops here, including ones that sell the folded-paper items that are burned ceremoniously in temples as offerings to comfort the dead. It is also where the **Sampeng Lane Market** begins. Turn right off Soi Isara Nuphap into what is actually known as Soi Wanit 1. Just before you do so you will see the Kao (or Old) Market, which has been here for more than two centuries (the Mai or New Market is on the same street, closer to the junction with Charoen Krung Road). Sampeng Lane is the narrowest of alleyways that seems to go on for miles. Actually it is a normal-sized, if somewhat narrow roadway so crammed with stalls selling all manner of surprising, delightful and downright bizarre items (like the parts of snakes used in traditional Chinese medicine) that it seems almost claustrophobically enclosed. Always crammed with people, you will just have to join the slowly moving line and make your gradual way through the stalls.

Sampeng Lane Market

Tang To Kang Gold Shop

The Sampeng Lane Market runs through a number of city blocks. The cross streets are a good opportunity for a little breathing room, but be careful crossing the busy roadways. The first you come to will be Mangkon Road, where the famous Tang To Kang Gold Shop is located (at number 345 Soi Wanit 1). Founded in 1870, it is the oldest gold shop in the city and is named

Mangkon Road

in honour of its founder. His son was appointed jeweller to the royal court by Rama VI and he built this tall building in 1921 (originally five storeys, now seven). A decorative mix of European elements but with a distinctly Chinese accent. The decorative garudas are a symbol of the company's royal warrant.

The area between Sampeng Lane and the river is home to a wide variety of interesting buildings, everything from charming old shophouses to huge wooden warehouses. The narrow sois that criss-cross this part of town remain much as they must have been in the 19th century, when it was full of traders, pawnbrokers and prostitutes. Although it is a busy area, particularly with trucks transporting goods to and from the nearby Ratchawong Pier, a wander around the streets and sois can be very rewarding as you will get to see a cross-section of Bangkok life that you'll not be likely to find anywhere else in the city. The charming shophouse at the corner of Songwat and Ratchawong Roads was built around 1900 and is a rather odd looking gothic style and has some fine fretwork on the balconies and over the point-arched windows.

Chinatown

Nakorn Kasem Market

Return to the Sampeng Lane Market and continue moving through it until you come to Chakkrawat Road and turn right. The Nakorn Kasem Market will be on your left at the junction with Charoen Krung Road. This used to be known as the Thieves' Market because of the amount of stolen goods traded here, it has since reformed itself and is now home to a range of shops selling metal ware, ornaments and musical instruments. This whole part of Charoen Krung Road is filled with enticing smells wafting from the innumerable noodle stalls that line the pavement. (The nearby Saphan Han Market, a covered market along both sides of Khlong Ong Ang, specialises in electrical goods.)

Nakorn Kasem Market
Opening times: 8am to 8pm daily
Admission: free

Phahurat Market

Retrace your steps down Chakkrawat Road and turn right onto Soi Wanit 1 (Sampeng Lane) again. This roadway turns into Phahurat Road at the point where it meets Chakkaphet Road and you will see Phahurat Market on your left. Phahurat Road is Bangkok's Little India, and at its heart lies a traditional Indian bazaar, Phahurat Market, which offers all the sights, sounds and smells

Siri Guru Singh Sabha

of a typical Indian city market. The stalls spill out onto the pavement of Chakkaphet Road selling a huge range of fabrics — everything from tableware to wedding outfits. The somewhat claustrophobic upstairs section is devoted to traditional Indian accessories such as sandals and jewellery, invariably ornate, while in the streets surrounding the market you can find tiny Indian restaurants and food stalls.

To the rear of the market is located the **Siri Guru Singh Sabha,** a traditional Sikh temple and one of the most important spiritual places for Bangkok's large Indian community. This beautifully decorative four-storey building is topped by a gilded dome and is said to be the second largest Sikh temple outside India. The temple's most sacred shrine is located on the very top floor, in a spacious hallway strewn with rich oriental rugs. Remember to cover your head before entering the temple.

Phahurat Market
Opening times: 9am to 6pm daily
Admission: free

Siri Guru Singh Sabha
Opening times: 8am to 5pm daily
Admission: free

Chinatown

Shophouse,
Ban Mo Road

Flower Market

Turn left on leaving Phahurat Market and follow Phahurat Road until it turns into Phra Phitak Road. Then take the next left onto Ban Mo Road, which contains a charming terrace of neoclassical shophouses running nearly all the way along its right-hand side. Nearly all are in quite bad shape but they illustrate just how high the standard of Bangkok's architecture was in the nineteenth century. At the end of Ban Mo Road turn right and you will see the Flower Market, known as Pak Khlong Market on your left. This 24-hour flower market overlooking Chakkaphet Road is also famous for having the widest variety of flowers on sale in the kingdom. Deliveries begin to arrive around 1am and by dawn the display features a bewildering array of different types of bloom, even tulips from the Netherlands. Apart from providing the city with wholesale flowers, the market also stocks fresh vegetables. It is also possible to buy the flowers individually, in bouquets, or arranged in baskets. The best time to visit this market is around 9am when there is the widest possible choice of blossoms on display.

Flower Market
Opening times: 24 hours daily
Admission: free

Link to the Rattanakosin walk:
Follow Chakkaphet Road across Khlong Lord and take a right up Sanam Chai Road and you will see the Siam Discovery Museum on your left.

Rattanakosin

Nearest Chao Phraya Express Pier: Rachinee
Approximate walking time: 2 hours

Historic Royal City

This is the heart of the old city of Bangkok. Known as Rattanakosin in English and Phra Nakhon in Thai, this was the centre of the new capital founded by Rama I in 1782 and is full of temples, palaces and museums. It is the spiritual and historic heart of the city, and contains some of Thailand's finest Rattanakosin-style architecture (a mixture of Thai and Western elements that takes its name from this part of the city), the best example being the Grand Palace itself, the grounds of which are also home to Wat Phra Kaeo, home to the country's most venerated image, the Emerald Buddha.

THE WALK

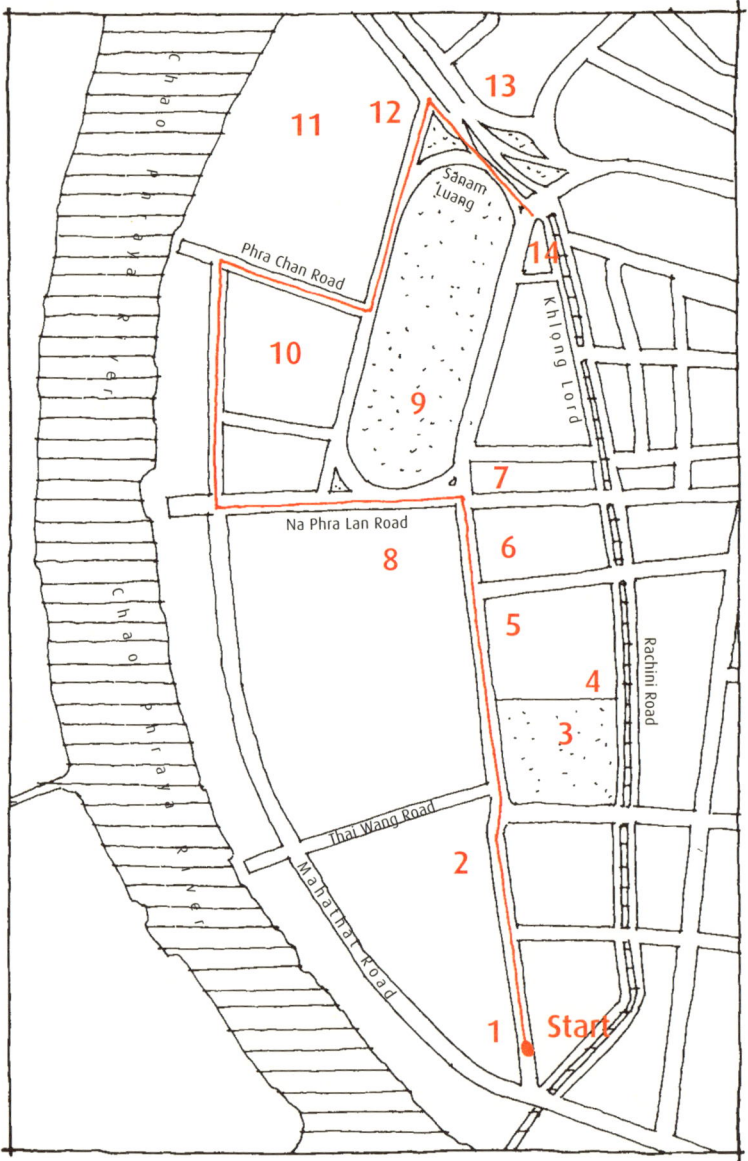

11
12
13
Chao Phraya River
Sanam Luang
Phra Chan Road
10
9
14
Khlong Lord
7
Na Phra Lan Road
8
6
5
Rachini Road
4
3
Thai Wang Road
2
Mahathai Road
1 Start
Chao Phraya River

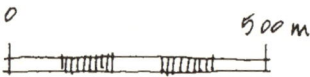

0   500 m

KEY

1. Siam Discovery Museum
2. Wat Pho
3. Saran Rom Park
4. Wat Ratchapradit
5. Saran Rom Palace
6. Ministry of Defence
7. Lak Muang Shrine
8. Grand Palace
9. Sanam Luang
10. Wat Mahathat
11. National Museum
12. National Theatre
13. National Gallery
14. Mae Toranee Fountain

Rattanakosin

Siam Discovery Museum

If you are walking from the Rachinee Chao Phraya Express Pier, walk up Rachinee Alley, cross the junction with Maharat Road and walk up Sanam Chai Road and you will come to the Siam Discovery Museum on your left at number 4. Housed in the former Ministry of Commerce, this handsome neoclassical building dates from 1922 and was one of the first office buildings in the country. The magnificent main staircase is cantilevered and the loggias across the first floor are lovely and airy. This interesting museum opened in 2008 and attempts to explain what it means to be Thai via a series of interactive multimedia displays and tableaux that show the Thai people's long history and highlights the Khmer, Sukhothai and Ayutthayan periods.

Siam Discovery Museum

Opening times: 10am to 6pm, Tue–Sun
Admission charges

> **Did You Know?**
> The 'Royal Mile', as the stretch of river that skirts Rattanakosin is known, is actually a canal. It was built in 1534 as a shortcut to eliminate the oxbow which is now known as Khlong Bangkok Noi, and to make it easier for foreign ships to trade with the old capital of Ayutthaya.

Wat Pho

Continue along Sanam Chai Road you will come to Wat Pho on your left. Best known as a school for traditional Thai massage, Wat Pho is also a renowned centre for traditional medicine. Officially known in Thai as Wat Phra Chetuphon, foreigners seem to have clung to their abbreviation of its old name, Wat Photaram. Its other name in English is the Temple of the Reclining Buddha, from the serene statue which also happens to be the largest reclining Buddha in the country (one of about 800 Buddha statues in the complex). This is Bangkok's oldest and largest temple and was originally built back in the sixteenth century. In the 1780s Rama I rebuilt it and enlarged the complex. His grandson, Rama III, built the Chapel of the Reclining Buddha in 1832 in the classic Rattanakosin style to house this impressive image, and it was he who turned the temple into a place of learning. Today it is one of Thailand's foremost centres for public education. It has a lively yet lived-in grandeur, but the temple's very popularity detracts from any feeling of reverence the visitor might have been expecting to find here, all the same it is a pleasant complex to ramble in and contains some fine details, such as excellent paintings as well as numerous statues of soldiers guarding doorways, which originally came from China as ballast for ships and were presented by the merchants to the temple as a way of making merit. The monks themselves, some 300 or so of them, live across Chetuphon Road in the temple monastery.

Wat Pho

Wat Pho
Opening times: 8am to 5pm daily
Admission charges

Wat Pho Massage School
Opening times: 10am to 6pm daily
Admission charges

Note: Thai Massage
Supposedly dating back 2,500 years, traditional Thai massage is related to
Chinese acupuncture and Indian yoga. Wat Pho founded a massage school in
the 1960s which has since become the best-known in the city. The temple's
highly trained masseurs are skilled in the tough pulling and stretching of the
body's limbs that is the hallmark of Thai massage. Visitors can experience a
massage themselves or learn how to practice it on others via the courses,
held in Thai and English, at the temple.

Rattanakosin

Saran Rom Park

Continue along Sanam Chai Road and you will pass the imposing edifice of the **Territorial Defence Command** on your right. Completed in 1924, this robust neoclassical building commands the corner junction with Cheroen Krung Road and its impressive entrance portico consists of large-scale fluted Ionic columns. Built as an army barracks, the Thai reserve army's command has been located here since the 1950s. The building is also home to a small museum. Facing the Territorial Defence Command across Cheroen Krung Road is one of the entrances to **Saran Rom Park**. This is shaded by a cluster of ancient-looking banyan trees decorated as colourful shrines. This was originally the garden of nearby Saran Rom Palace and the park was home to a zoo in the nineteenth century but it closed down when the one at Dusit opened. Full of bridges and pools, there is also a decorative cast-iron fountain with water-spouting cherubs. The park is also home to a Thai-style **Drum Tower**, originally built in 1782 (but rebuilt a number of times since). This used to sound dawn and dusk and was also used as a warning against fire and enemy attack. There is also a **Clock Tower**, a mix of Western and Asian styles, and a **Chinese pagoda**, originally built in the Grand Palace Compound but moved here later. The park's most moving monument is a lovely Khmer-style memorial to Queen Sunanda who drowned in the river in 1880 despite being a good swimmer (no one dared to help her because it was forbidden for commoners to touch royalty).

Saran Rom Park
Opening times: 5am to 8pm daily
Admission: free

Pagoda, Saran Rom Park

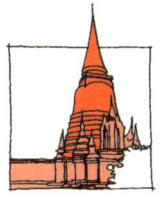

BRACKEN MAY '01

Rattanakosin

Wat Ratchapradit

Continue up Sanam Chai Road and turn right down Saran Rom Road and you will come to Wat Ratchapradit on your right towards the end. This is an intimate little temple on a small compound. Built in 1864 by Rama IV and owing to its royal connection it contains some very fine buildings, including the Grand Vihara, which has the royal seal on its pediment, and an interior mural depicting the king's visit to Prachuab Kiri Khan to observe the solar eclipse in 1868 (which is where he contracted the malaria which killed him). There is a life-sized statue of the king in a Khmer-style pavilion to the west of the Grand Vihara.

Wat Ratchapradit
Opening times: 5am to 10pm daily
Admission: free

Saran Rom Palace

Return to Sanam Chai Road and turn right and the Saran Rom Palace complex will be on your right. An imposing neoclassical building with baroque flourishes, it was built for Rama IV in the 1860s and intended to be the home of the crown prince but because the king unexpectedly died his son never had the chance to live here (one of his younger brothers moved in instead).

The building became the Ministry of Foreign Affairs for about two years in the 1880s but reverted into a palace for another crown prince, Rama VI, who moved out when he became king and so it was used to entertain visiting dignitaries before returning to use as a ministry in the 1920s. Almost demolished to make way for a multi-storey office building in the 1960s, part of the eastern wing of the palace was torn down but was rebuilt in 2007. The statue under the elaborate canopy on the plaza in front of the palace is of the original builder, Rama IV.

Located just behind the palace, on Kalayana Maitri Road, is the **Royal Thai Survey Department**, another long, low neoclassical building. Originally the Royal Military Academy established by Rama V in 1887, this moved away in 1909 and the building became home to the Army Chief of Staff before being made over to the Royal Thai Survey in 1931 (which had been established in 1885). The building was built in the early 1890s in a somewhat heavy neoclassicism, with oversized porches featuring Tuscan columns. The central one sports Rama V's crest.

Ministry of Defence

Return to Sanam Chai Road and the Ministry of Defence will be on your right. There used to be three palaces here. These were demolished in the nineteenth century to make way for a silk factory, among other things, then

Rama V decided to build the Thai Army's headquarters here in the 1880s. This vast square building, ranged around two interior courtyards, was also home to an arsenal and a barracks and it was the largest building in the city when it was built. Painted bright yellow, with white detailing on the column capitals and window surrounds, the main entrance consists of a vast porch where six Tuscan columns support a heavy balcony. The lawn in front of the building is home to the **Cannon Museum**, which includes some artillery that looks as if it's seen some action.

Cannon Museum
Opening times: 24 hours daily
Admission: free

Lak Muang Shrine
Continue along Sanam Chai Road and you will come to the Lak Muang Shrine on your right overlooking the corner where Lak Muang Road enters Sanam Luang. Also known as the City Pillar Shrine, this is home to Bangkok's guardian spirits — all Thai cities have such shrines. It is also where all distances from Bangkok are measured. The shrine consists of two monuments; the shorter one is original and was established here in 1782 at the astrologically auspicious time for the founding of the city. The taller shrine, a Khmer-style *prang*, originally stood in Thonburi but was moved here when Thonburi was incorporated into Greater Bangkok. The complex is also home to a Rattanakosin-style pavilion which dates from 1853. It was restored in the 1980s and again in 2006. People come here to pray and offer flowers; it is particularly popular with childless couples. Classical dancers also perform thanksgiving dances for good fortune attributed to the shrine.

Lak Muang Shrine
Opening times: 5am to 7pm daily
Admission: free

Grand Palace
Facing out over the southern end of Sanam Luang is Bangkok's most popular tourist attraction, the Grand Palace. This vast complex was established in 1782 and is home to a number of royal residences and throne halls as well as government offices and the Temple of the Emerald Buddha. The complex covers an area of approximately 160 hectares (65 acres) and is surrounded by a wall measuring just under two kilometres (about 1.25 miles). Originally the site was home to a seventeenth-century French fort, at a time when the previous royal palace and its administrative buildings were located across

Rattanakosin

the river in Thonburi. The French were forced to relinquish their stronghold in 1688 when it was discovered that they had been trying to convert the king to Christianity. The area surrounding the fort had also been home to a large Chinese community, who were forced to move when the area was designated for a new palace. The king chose this site because he considered it easier to defend from attacks by the Burmese. The Chinese were forced to move down the river, to what is now known as Chinatown.

The Grand Palace complex was built to be a self-sufficient city within a city, one the king need never leave. He could show himself from time to time on the specially constructed balcony overlooking Sanam Chai Road. The royal family no longer lives in the Grand Palace, they moved to the newer Chitrlada Palace in the Dusit district in the early 20th century. The **Grand Palace Hall** (Chakri Maha Prasat) was a royal residence constructed to celebrate the centenary of the ruling family in 1882. A hybrid of Thai and Western architectural styles, it is probably the best example of the Rattanakosin style in the country. In fact, because it was considered too demeaning to have a European-style building at the heart of the complex, the three-tiered pagoda over the centre was added at the last minute. With your back to the Grand Palace Hall you will see the **Amarin Vinitchai Throne Hall** on your right. Also originally built as a royal

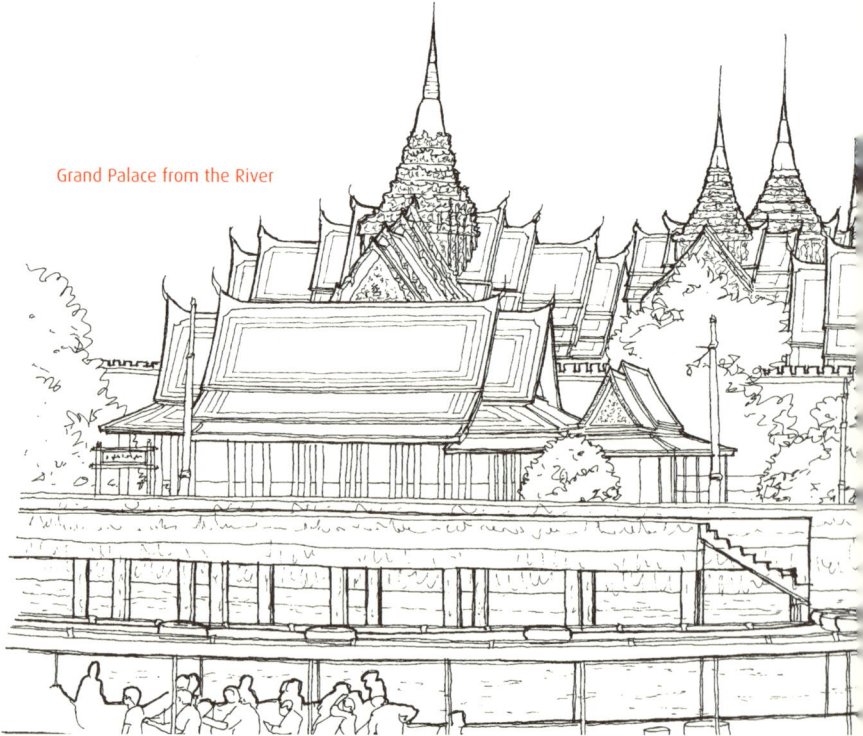

Grand Palace from the River

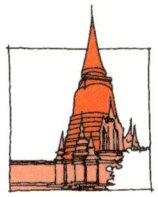

residence but now only used for the most important royal and ceremonial occasions, such as coronations. The building contains Rama I's bedchamber, which is where each new Thai monarch must spend his first night after being crowned.

Facing this across the square in front of the Grand Palace Hall is **Dusit Maha Prasit** (Dusit Hall), which is where the bodies of deceased kings are laid in state prior to cremation. The complex is also home to a **Weapons Museum**, a **Coins and Decorations Museum** and the **Wat Phra Kaeo Museum** (which is not in the same place as the temple of the same name but is worth a visit).

Wat Phra Kaeo itself (the Temple of the Emerald Buddha) is Thailand's holiest temple and is home to the country's most sacred image, the Emerald Buddha (Phra Kaeo). Although this complex is referred to as a wat (a monastery) no monks actually live here. It was completed in time for Bangkok's centenary in 1882 and formed a focal point for the celebrations. The Emerald Buddha itself is housed in a lavishly decorated bot, surrounded by 112 *garudas* which are shown holding *nagas* and are typical of the temple's dazzling decorative details. The upper terrace of Wat Phra Kaeo contains many beautifully gilded figures of Aponsi. Eight *prangs* border the east of the temple, while the Ramakien Gallery, extending clockwise all around the

Doorway detail, Grand Palace

Rattanakosin

Grand Palace

cloisters, consists of 178 panels depicting the entire story of the Ramakien. The temple's gates are flanked by pairs of king demon statues, there are 12 in total. The complex also contains a beautiful stone model of Angkor Wat, which was ordered by Rama IV, but only completed during the reign of his successor. (From 1769, when King Taksin annexed the provinces of Siam Reap and Battambang, until 1907, when these provinces were ceded to France, Angkor was actually a part of Thailand.)

Grand Palace
Opening times: 8:30am to 3:30pm daily
Admission charges (which covers Vimarnmek Palace as well)

Wat Phra Kaeo
Opening times: 8:30am to 3:30pm daily
Admission included as part of the Grand Palace

Did You Know?
The king's harem was housed in a secluded corner of the Grand Palace complex guarded by an elite force of female guards.

Note: The Emerald Buddha

Thailand's holiest image was brought to Wat Phra Kaeo on 5 March 1785 by a grand procession which began across the river at Wat Arun, where it had been kept for the previous 15 years. The first mention of the statue was in 1434 when lightning struck the chedi of Wat Phra Kaeo in Chiang Rai, Northern Thailand, revealing a simple stucco image. The abbot of the temple then kept it in his residence until some of the plaster flaked off revealing a jadeite image underneath. The King of Chiang Mai, hearing about the image, sent an army of elephants to retrieve it, unfortunately for the king the animal that was carrying the Emerald Buddha refused to go in the direction of Chiang Mai, and the entourage, taking this as a sign, decided to go to Lampang instead. The image moved a number of times during the following century, eventually ending up in Wat Pha Kaew, Laos in 1552, where it remained until General Chakri (later King Rama I) captured Vientiane in 1778 and took it back to Thailand.

Sanam Luang

Sanam Luang

One of Bangkok city centre's few open spaces, this 'field of kings' is the venue for important national ceremonies, such as the royal ploughing ceremony, royal cremations, and the annual kite-flying festival. Rama V was a keen kite-flyer and was glad to allow Sanam Luang to be used for this sport. Fiercely contested kite fights still take place here between February and April. Lined with ancient-looking tamarind trees and surrounded by imposing buildings, including the Grand Palace, the National Museum, National Theatre and National Art Gallery, the Ministry of Justice, two universities and an important temple, Sanam Luang also has a more down-to-earth side, with hawkers on the neighbouring streets selling lotions and amulets, and palm readers and astrologers casting horoscopes. It also used to be home to the weekend market before it moved to the broader pastures of Chatuchak to the north.

Facing the Grand Palace compound across Na Phra Lan Road is a lovely row of decorative neoclassical shophouses and **Silpakorn University**, which

Rattanakosin

is Thailand's most famous fine art school. Founded by Italian artist Corrado Feroci in 1943, the campus includes part of a palace that dates from the reign of Rama I. A small bookshop just inside the gates stocks books on Thai art in English, while the university often holds art shows in its exhibition hall — the notice boards outside the entrance show details and opening times. Walk to the end of Na Phra Lan Road and the area around Chang Pier contains some more fine shophouses, now rare in Bangkok but very attractive. One of these is a branch of the **Thanachart Bank**, a handsome Dutch-gabled building with some lovely Art Nouveau decorative panels. Sympathetically restored, it is still in use as a bank.

Silpakorn University Hall of Sculpture
Opening times: 8:30am to 4:30pm, Mon–Fri
Admission: free

Did You Know?
Sanam Luang is regarded as one of the luckiest places in the city because it is home to the Grand Palace, the Lak Muang (City Pillar) Shrine and the Amulet Market.

Shophouses, Na Phra Lan Road

The Chao Phraya River is one of the most important transport arteries in the city for goods and produce as well as for people. Tiny boats laden with all sorts of cargo race across it daily, zipping past the huge rice barges, and competing with the numerous ferries for space at the jetties. No visitor can really understand Bangkok until they've seen it from the river, and one of the best and cheapest ways to do this is to catch the Chao Phraya Express. There are also any number of cross-river ferries, as well as plenty of long-tail boats which can be hired privately and make for a good way to see the city's complicated web of khlongs.

Wat Mahathat

With your back to the river, turn left onto Maharat Road where hawkers sell an amazing variety of religious trinkets in the Amulet Market that takes place on the pavement on both sides of the road all the way from the corner of the Grand Palace compound to Thammasat University. The entrance to Wat Mahathat, which is also known as the Temple of the Great Relic, is about halfway down Maharat Road and on your right-hand side. This temple is the national centre for the Mahanakai monastic sect, and its compound contains one of Bangkok's two Buddhist universities. Meditation classes are also held here near the monks' quarters. There is also a traditional herbal medicine market, and a weekend market. A large complex, it is more notable for its atmosphere, which is beautifully serene, than for its architecture. It was built during the reign of Rama I, and the *wihan* and *bot* were both rebuilt between

Mondop, Wat Mahathat

Rattanakosin

97

1844 and 1851. The *mondop*, which contains the famous relic that gives the temple its name, has a cruciform roof, a feature not often found in Bangkok's temples.

At the end of Maharat Road, across Phra Chan Alley, sits the **Thammasat University** complex. Founded in 1933, it is well-known for its law and political science faculties, it was also the scene of bloody student riots in the 1970s. The grounds are home to a Memorial Sculpture Garden, a controversial reminder of those violent times (something that can be seen from the fact that work on this garden did not begin until the 1990s). The university's best-known building is the Administration Building, also known as the **Dome Building** (with, confusingly, a spire). This dates from the late 1930s and looks out over this stretch of the river. Return to Phra Chan Alley and turn left and continue through the open-air **Amulet Market** which doesn't just limit itself to these ever-popular trinkets but sells all kinds of religious (sometimes quite odd-looking) paraphernalia.

Wat Mahathat
Opening times: 7am to 8pm daily
Admission: free

Note: Amulets
Thais can be highly superstitious, and many of them wear amulets as a form of protection. These come in a wide variety of forms and sizes and are sold in specialist markets, often near spiritually significant sites. There are even a number of magazines devoted to them. Although many are religious in nature, tiny images of the Buddha or some other statue are common, others are more straightforward, such as miniature phalluses, meant to aid fertility.

Amulet Market

National Museum

Continue along Phra Chan Road until you get to Sanam Luang and turn left and you will come to the National Museum on your left near the end of Sanam Luang. The museum's collection was begun by Rama IV. He began to display rare and interesting objects in the Grand Palace from 1874 but rehoused them in the Wang Na (Front Palace) in 1887 — the basis for this museum. The palace itself dates from the early 1780s and is now home to one of the largest and most comprehensive collections of art and sculpture in Southeast Asia, with every period of Thai history represented.

The museum provides an excellent introduction to the arts, crafts and history of the country. Apart from the old Wang Na palace (which houses a varied collection of everything from ancient weapons to shadow puppets) there is also the Buddhaisawan Chapel, which dates from 1787 and is particularly worth seeing, not only for its architecture but because it contains the Phra Buddha Sing (after the Emerald Buddha, the most venerated Buddha image in Thailand and decorated with some of the best Rattanakosin-style murals in the country). Other attractions include galleries of history and prehistory, and the Royal Funeral Chariots Gallery. The frequent guided tours are good and included in the entrance fee.

National Museum
Opening times: 9am to 4pm, Wed-Sun
Admission charges

National Theatre

Occupying a large, landscaped corner overlooking Sanam Luang beside the National Museum is the 500-seat **National Theatre** which specialises in Thai theatrical productions. Despite being built in the middle of the 1960s the building itself incorporates several traditional Thai architectural touches, particularly some Rattanakosin-style detailing. The site used to be part of the grounds of Wang Na Palace. Facing the theatre and museum across Na Phra That Alley sits a **War Memorial** commemorating those Thai combatants who died for the Allied cause in World War I. Built in 1921, this chedi-like structure was designed by a prince who was also an architect.

National Gallery

On the other side of Somdet Phra Pin Klao Road from the war memorial is the **National Gallery**. This attractive building was originally built as the Royal Mint in 1902 (when it moved from the Grand Palace). The mint then moved again around 1968 and the building became home to the National Art Gallery in the 1970s. Its collection consists mainly of modern Thai and international

Rattanakosin

War Memorial and
National Theatre

art. Its gracious, well-proportioned rooms also frequently host the work of prominent Asian artists in the form of temporary exhibitions. The road onto which the gallery looks, Somdet Phra Pin Klao, is now the elevated approach to the Phra Pin Klao Bridge, which was built in the early 1970s, before that it used to be Khlong Lord. Sadly, this stretch of the canal was covered when the bridge was built.

National Gallery
Opening times: 9am to 4pm, Wed-Sun
Admission charges

National Art Gallery

Note: Khlong Lord

This is the innermost of the three concentric canals dug for Bangkok's defences by King Rama I. Khlong Lord turned Rattanakosin into an island and even though the waterway is no longer visible north of Sanam Luang, it emerges from its culvert at the Mae Thoranee Fountain and runs due south, passing the Ministries of Justice, Defence and Foreign Affairs as well as Wat Rajapradit, a tiny temple founded in 1864 and built on a foundation consisting of old water jars, before flowing back into the Chao Phraya River at the Rachinee Ferry Pier. To walk along the banks of this canal is to walk through the very oldest part of the city.

Mae Toranee Fountain

Return to Sanam Luang and follow it as it veers around to the right and you will come to the Mae Toranee Fountain on your left. Originally built by Queen Saovapha (wife of Rama V) to provide fresh drinking water, this statue depicts the earth goddess Mae Toranee and illustrates an ancient Buddhist legend popular in temple murals. The story goes that while the Buddha was sitting in meditation, Mara, the force of evil, sent a host of demons to offer him earthly

Rattanakosin

temptations. He remained cross-legged and pointed his right hand towards the ground (the most frequently seen pose of the Buddha in Thailand) and called upon the earth goddess to vouch for his numerous good deeds which had earned him an ocean of water stored in the earth. Mae Toranee obliged by wringing out her hair, the resultant flow of water engulfed Mara's demons.

Mae Toranee Fountain

Link to Bang Lamphoo walk:

Leave the Mae Toranee Fountain and follow Khlong Lord on your left until you come to the bridge at Kalayang Maitri Road and turn left. Follow this as it turns into Bamrung Muang Road and you will see the Giant Swing directly ahead of you.

Bang Lamphoo

Old City Centre

This area takes its name from the second of three concentric canals dug for Bangkok's defences by King Rama I. Khlong Bang Lamphoo is much less-preserved than Khlong Lord, the innermost of the three canals, but it is still a pleasant waterway. The area is also home to some of Thailand's most spectacular temples as well as the Golden Mount, which used to be the highest point in the city. It is now best known for being the haunt of backpackers, with numerous cheap hotels, shops and restaurants all clustered around the near-legendary Khao San Road, as well as the newer, trendier district near the river on Phra Athit Road, a wonderful place for restaurants and cafés.

THE WALK

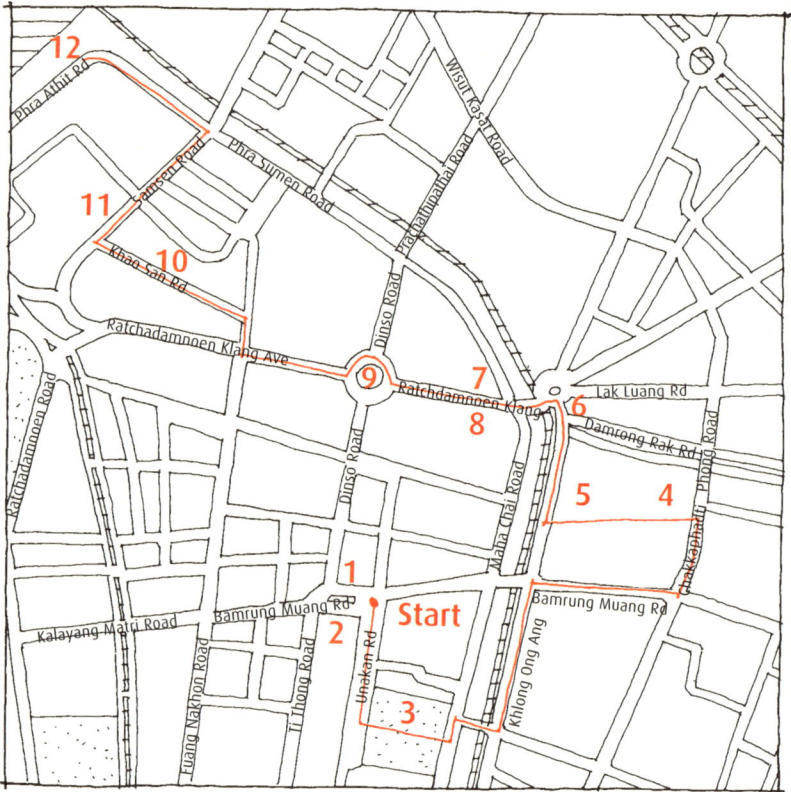

0   500 m

KEY

1. Giant Swing
2. Wat Suthat
3. Romaneerat Park
4. Wat Saket
5. Golden Mount
6. King Prajadhipok Museum
7. Queen's Gallery
8. Loha Prasat
9. Democracy Monument
10. Khao San Road
11. Wat Chana Songkram
12. Phra Athit Road

Bang Lamphoo

Giant Swing

If you are walking from the Chang Chao Phraya Express Pier, follow Na Phra Lan Road, then turn right at the corner of the Grand Palace compound and left onto Kalayang Maitri Road. Follow it as it turns into Bamrung Muang Road (originally an old elephant trail out of the city) and you will see the Giant Swing directly in front of you.

Sao Ching Cha, as the Giant Swing is known in Thai, was originally built in 1784 by King Rama I and was twice the height of this more recent replica. During ceremonies, which were Brahmin in origin, teams of four would swing up to 180 degrees while one of them would try to catch a sack of gold in their teeth. The event, linked to the veneration of Shiva, caused many deaths and was finally abolished in the 1930s.

The huge plaza to the right of the swing is the Bangkok Metropolitan Administration Plaza, at the top of which sits **Bangkok City Hall**, rather an intimidating-looking building built by a local architect in the 1950s. The point-arched screen was added in the early 1960s. A long plaque near the Giant Swing contains Bangkok's name written in Thai in gold lettering; you can see why it is the world's longest city name.

Wat Suthat

Facing the other side of the Giant Swing from the plaza is Wat Suthat. Less visited than Wat Pho, this is in fact a much more impressive temple. Begun in 1807 by Rama I, and decorated by his son, it wasn't finally completed until the reign of the grandson, Rama III. The artwork and architecture are excellent examples of the Rattanakosin style. The central Buddha, at eight metres, is one of the largest surviving Sukhothai bronzes and was moved to Bangkok from Wat Mahathat in Sukhothai by Rama I. The wihan, which

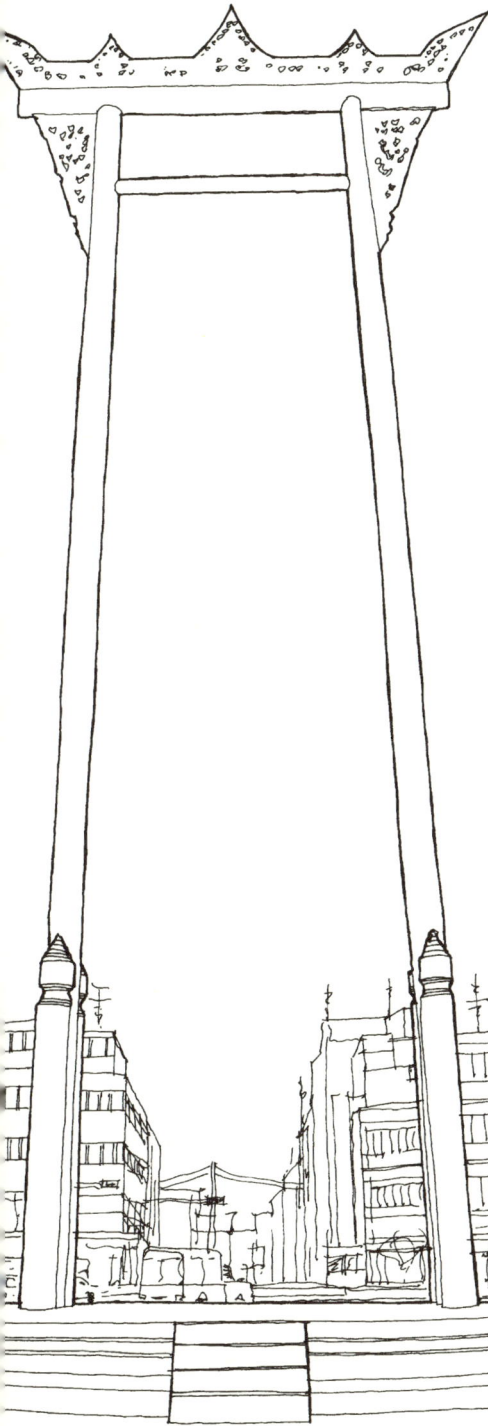

Giant Swing

Wat Suthat

is the largest in the city, as well as the tallest, is also regarded as the most elegant in terms of its design and it contains murals that are among the most celebrated in the country. Amazingly intricate, they depict the Traiphum (Buddhist cosmology) and were restored in the 1980s. The teak doors to the *wihan* are also noteworthy, carved in five delicate layers and standing five-and-a-half-metres tall, one of them, supposedly carved by Rama II himself, was moved to the National Museum. The cloister outside the *wihan* is lined with 156 golden Buddha images, the statuary said to have been brought to Bangkok as ballast in ships carrying rice to China. The *wihan* and *bot* are often closed to the public but the rest of the complex is pleasant to wander in and is home to an amazing variety of statuary of all shapes and forms.

Wat Suthat
Opening times: 8:30am to 9pm daily
Admission charges

Romaneerat Park

Leave Wat Suthat and turn right onto Siri Phong Road and the **Dev Mandir Temple**, a Hindu Brahmin place of worship, will be on your left. Also known as the Hindu Samaj, this modern and not particularly interesting-looking building is the centre of Bangkok's Brahmin devotees. The compound is also home to the Bharat Vidyalaya School. Though Brahmanism has been an integral part of Thai royal life since the fourteenth century (Brahmin priests are still central to certain court functions), few temples in Bangkok exclusively honour the

Hindu Trinity of Brahma, Shiva and Vishnu. Brahmanism might seem to be an anachronism in a Buddhist royal court but is explained by the fact that they originally came to Ayutthaya from Angkor after the Thai conquest of the Khmer capital, and the Ayutthayan kings, in trying to rule a Khmer empire, took over these rites to legitimise their claim to power.

Continue along Siri Phong Road and you will come to **Romaneerat Park** on your left. This used to be Bangkok's main prison. Closed down in the 1990s, five of the compound's watchtowers still remain, as do some of the original buildings, one of which, a lovely symmetrical neoclassical edifice facing Maha Chai Road and dating from 1890, is now the **Corrections Museum.** This contains gruesome but fascinating exhibits, including artefacts and wax models showing methods of execution past and present, it even has early twentieth-century photographs showing a beheading. The park itself is peaceful and well laid out and provides excellent views of Wat Suthat.

Romaneerat Park
Opening times: 5am to 9pm daily
Admission: free

Corrections Museum
Opening times: 8:30am to 4:30pm, Mon–Fri
Admission: free

Watchtower, Romaneerat Park

Bang Lamphoo

Wat Saket

Leave the Corrections Museum by turning left onto Maha Chai Road and take a right onto Luang Road. Cross the canal and take the next left up Boriphat Road and you will pass the **Monks' Bowl Village,** a cluster of narrow alleyways where the traditional alms bowls used by Buddhist monks are still made in the time-honoured tradition of beating eight pieces of metal together using small hammers before enamelling. Continue along Boriphat Road until you come to Bamrung Muang Road and turn right. On your right at the junction with Chakkaphadti Phong Road you will see the round water towers of the **Maen Si Pumping Station** peeking over the elegant Edwardian office building on the corner. Built in 1914 to supply clean water to the city; the water was filtered here after being pumped from the Chao Phraya River upstream. The waterworks moved out in the 1990s and there are plans to turn this pretty complex of well-maintained buildings into a library or community arts centre.

With your back to the Maen Si Pumping Station walk up Chakkaphadti Phong Road and you will see **Wat Saket** on your left. Visitors to this temple usually come to climb the Golden Mount, an artificial hill topped with a golden tower. Most skip the temple building itself, which is a pity as it is rather beautiful, sitting as it does in an attractively laid out compound. It is also one of the oldest temples in Bangkok. Built during the Ayutthaya period, it was originally called Wat Sakae and was significantly rebuilt by Rama I in the late eighteenth century. It is said that Rama I, when he was still General Chakri, stopped here in 1782 on his way back from Laos with the Emerald Buddha and ceremonially bathed before proceeding to Thonburi where he

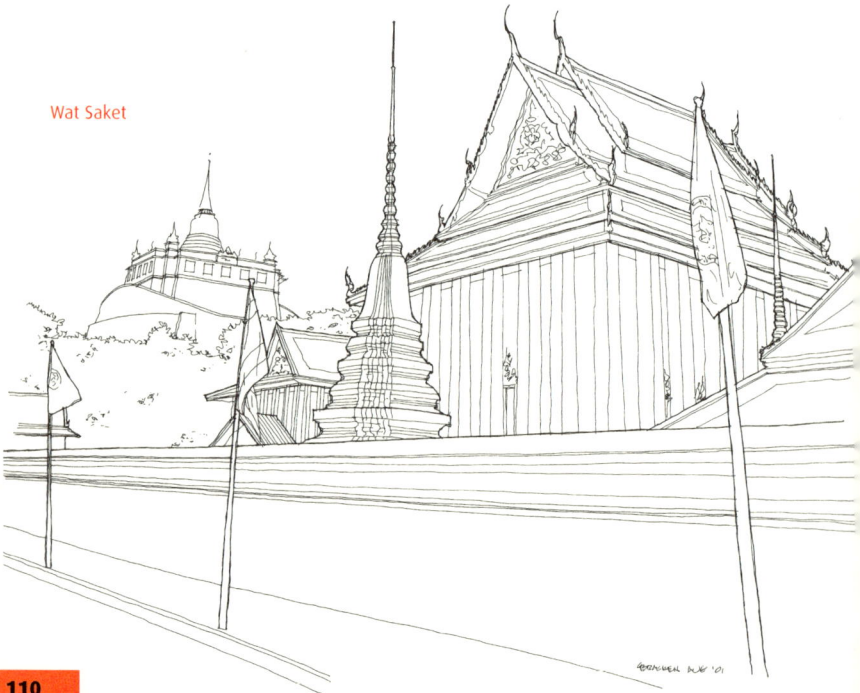

Wat Saket

was crowned king. The temple's name subsequently changed to Saket, which means 'the washing of hair'. During the 19th century the temple's grounds, being just outside the city walls, were used as a crematorium, particularly during epidemics. During the reign of Rama II one such epidemic killed more than 30,000 people, their bodies were taken out of the city via the Pratu Pii (Ghost Gate) and laid here. Too many to be cremated, they soon attracted dogs and vultures. There were epidemics in Bangkok every ten years or so until about 1900, each killing around 10,000 people. The grounds are now used for more pleasant purposes, being home to an annual fair in November, with dancing and candlelit processions.

Wat Saket
Opening times: 8am to 5pm daily
Admission: free

Did You Know?
Rama V prohibited torture to extract confessions but one of the methods had been to force the accused inside a rattan ball which contained spikes, this was then kicked around by elephants.

Pavilion,
Golden Mount

Bang Lamphoo

Golden Mount

Behind Wat Saket sits the Golden Mount. Rama III, inspired by a dream, attempted to build a huge brick pyramid here with a *prang* on top but the soft soil of the city soon led to its collapse. His descendant Rama IV restarted work on it the 1850s, when the necessary technology had become available, and he created the 80-metre mound seen today. The sanctuary at the top houses relics of the Buddha presented to Rama V by the Viceroy of India. The long curved staircase is lined with fascinating monuments and tombs, some of which are quite grand. The climb itself is arduous but the views from the top are worth it, as they take in the whole of the original city centre, including the Grand Palace, Wat Pho and even Wat Arun across the river. It is still the highest point in this part of Bangkok and was, until the 1960s, the highest point in the whole of the city, it has since been dwarfed by numerous skyscrapers but fortunately there don't happen to be any nearby.

Golden Mount
Opening times: 7:30am to 5:30pm daily
Admission charges

King Prajadhipok Museum

Exit the Golden Mount compound onto Boriphat Road and turn right. This street is full of traditional Thai woodworkers. Follow the road until you come to Khlong Mahanak and cross the **Mahadthai Uthit Bridge**, which was built by Rama VI in 1914 as a memorial to his father. Also known as the 'weeping bridge', it is decorated with beautifully carved bas-reliefs showing the Thai people mourning the loss of their king. Just after the bridge on your right is the **King Prajadhipok Museum.** King Prajadhipok (Rama VII) was Thailand's last absolute ruler before the military coup of 1932. This museum is housed in a delicately Italianate symmetrical building which commands a busy junction. Its centrally placed open cupola is particularly fine. Built in 1906 as a tailors specialising in court and military uniforms, the Public Works Department took it over in 1933, only moving out in 2001. Now a museum dedicated to the life of Rama VII, it displays photos, documents and some of his personal belongings showing his life from the time he was a schoolboy at Eton through his short reign to his abdication in 1935 (when he moved back to England).

King Prajadhipok Museum
Opening times: 9am to 4pm, Tue-Sun
Admission charges

Queen's Gallery

With your back to the King Prajadhipok Museum you will be facing the wide expanse of the **Phan Fa Bridge**, one of the city's most attractive. Consisting of a steel structure supporting concrete slabs, these are decorated with well-proportioned pillars, curved marble bases and elaborate wrought iron railings. Considerably wider than when it was first built in 1906, this is one of a number of bridges designed by Italian engineers built by the Department of Public Works. This one was paid for by Rama V personally. Its looks almost imperial, which is quite appropriate as it forms part of the impressive Ratchdamnoen Avenue which runs from here all the way to Sanam Luang in the west and the Ananta Samakorn Throne Hall in the north. Overlooking the bridge on the right is the **Queen's Gallery.** Established in 2003 in this five-storey neo-Brutalist concrete building, basically it is square-shaped in plan, with turreted corners. The building's curved protruding balconies give it an octagonal feel and may be a reference to the Mahakan Fort across the avenue. Its collection consists of modern and contemporary paintings mostly by local artists.

Queen's Gallery
Opening times: 10am to 7pm, Thur–Tue
Admission charges

Phan Fa Bridge and King Prajadhipok Museum

Bang Lamphoo

Loha Prasat

Facing the Queen's Gallery across Ratchdamnoen Avenue is the remains of **Mahakath Fort,** one of only two remaining in the city, the other is Phra Athit. This one takes its name from the Hindu god of death and still has some of its cannon. Restored as part of the city's bicentennial celebrations, as was part of the nearby city wall, plans to turn it into a park were resisted by the area's residents. Facing Mahakath Fort across Maha Chai Road is **Wat Ratchanatda**, a temple founded by Rama III and completed by Rama V. An impressive cluster of buildings, its most remarkable is the **Loha Prasat**, or 'metal palace'. Construction on this began in the 1840s and it is only the third metal prasat ever constructed (the first was in India about 500 BC, of which there is no trace, and the second in Sri Lanka in the third century, on which this one is based). This square three-tiered pyramid has 37 *mondops* to represent the 37 attributes of Buddhist enlightenment and are topped with hti. It was intended as a place for monks to meditate but was never used. Restoration began in the 1960s and was only completed in 2007. The forecourt in front of the temple is home to the **Mahachesdabodin Royal Pavilion**, the latest addition to a space that was formed when a popular cinema was knocked down in 1989. A pleasant enough space with planting and a monument to Rama III, but its chief contribution to the city is the opening up of the stunning profile of Loha Prasat.

Loha Prasat, Wat Ratchanatda
Opening times: 9am to 5pm daily
Admission charges

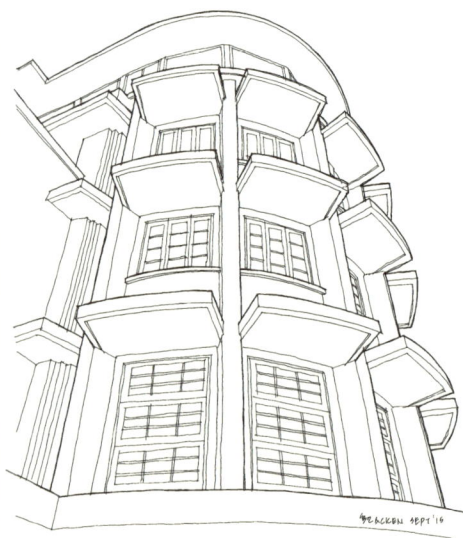

Art Deco corner building,
Ratchdamnoen Avenue

Democracy Monument

With your back to the Loha Prasat turn left onto Ratchdamnoen Avenue, which means 'royal passage'. Built in the early 20th century and modelled on the avenues of Paris, the buildings along it were only completed in the 1930s and 1940s by Field Marshall Phibul (Thailand's dictator during World War II) so these have an altogether more austere air (although some of them are quite attractive in their stripped-down Art Deco way). Quite a number have been painted yellow with white

Democracy Monument

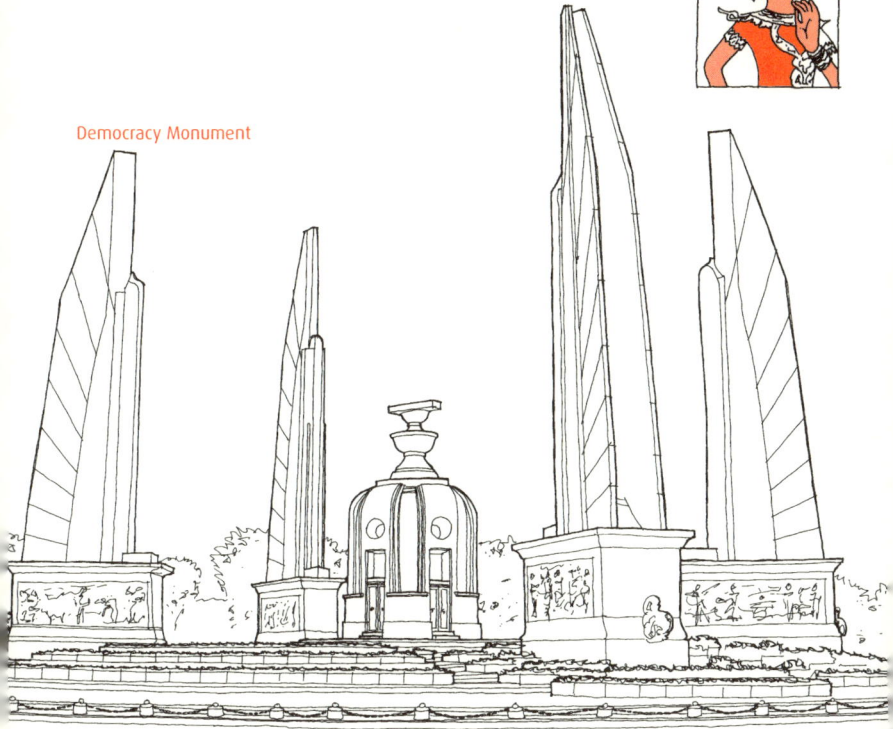

detailing, which has done much to brighten their appearance. One is now home to the **Ratchdamnoen Contemporary Art Centre** (number 84) which has been located here since 2013 and is part of the 2001 masterplan to revitalise the area. Its interior was stripped of its pokey partitions (from the days when it was an office) and are now light and spacious and cover four floors that feature some interesting contemporary art.

The Ratchdamnoen Contemporary Art Centre overlooks the wide circus around the **Democracy Monument**. Designed by Silpa Bhirasi, an Italian who became a Thai citizen and also adopted a Thai name, it was built in 1939 to commemorate the revolution of 1932 (when Thailand became a constitutional monarchy). It has become one of the focal points of Thailand's occasional pro-democracy demonstrations. Each of the monument's features signify some aspect of the revolutionary date, 24 June 1932. The four soaring Art Deco wing-like towers are 24 metres high and the 75 cannon indicate the Buddhist year 2475 (1932 AD). The pedestal, which contains a copy of the constitution, is three metres high and refers to the third month of the Thai calendar (June).

Ratchdamnoen Contemporary Art Centre
Opening times: 10am to 7pm, Tue–Sun
Admission: free

Bang Lamphoo

Khao San Road

Walk anti-clockwise around the Democracy Monument and you will pass a **McDonald's** which just happens to be housed in a long, low glass-fronted modernist building. Dating from 1943, the façade's gentle curve follows the circus of the Democracy Monument and is where the king's observation platform used to be located for watching army parades. Continue around the circus and onto Ratchdamnoen Avenue and you will come to Tanao Road on your right, this is where the **Bo Be Market** is located, one of the best for cloth in the city, especially Chinese silk. Follow Tanao Road and turn left onto Khao San Road. This one small street has become something of a legend, featuring in books and films. It has been a favourite with backpackers for decades and there are plenty of inexpensive guesthouses, not to mention bars and restaurants. The street has had something of a shift towards gentrification in recent years, certainly it is nothing as grimy (or cheap) as it was in the 1990s but it is still home to a number of market stalls that stock everything a traveller could possibly need, from boots and backpacks to tattoo parlours and even tailors. It also stocks a good range of second-hand books, ideal for long bus journeys up-country or trips out to the islands.

One of the signs of Khao San Road's creeping gentrification is **Khaosan Garden**, a pretty villa dating from 1910 located on the right just after Soi Sunset (walk through the archway). This is now home to an upmarket cluster of restaurants. The building itself is in good condition and sports Corinthian pilasters and some delicately carved fretwork.

Khao San Road

Street vendor, Khao San Rd

Wat Chana Songkram

Continue to the end of Khao San Road, turn right onto Chakrabongse Road and Wat Chana Songkram will be on your left. An elegantly simple temple built for Rama I's Mon allies and because they had helped him defeat the Burmese it was known as the War Victory Temple. A large compound which is also home to a modern Thai-style temple school and monks' quarters. Continue along Chakrabongse Road and you will come to the **Chakrabongse Mosque** which is approached off the small alleyway called Trok Surao (hidden behind some shophouses and a distance beyond Rambuttri Alley). Standing in a rather rundown-looking compound of wooden houses it dates from 1779. Originally wood, now rebuilt in brick and stucco, its style is Indo-Saracenic (a style popular with British colonial architects in Asia) and it sports an octagonal tower topped with an onion-shaped dome. This was the only mosque located within the old city walls and was where craftsmen and goldsmiths worshipped. They had come to work at the royal court after the annexation of the southern province of Pattani.

Phra Athit Road

Continue along Chakrabongse Road and turn left onto Phra Sumen Road and you will see the **Kuru Sapha Printing House** on your right near where the road curves to the left. This is one of the first modernist buildings in the city and dates from 1925. It was home to the Wat Sangwet Printing School until the mid-1940s and was where religious texts were printed. It became a government printing house in the 1950s, producing school textbooks for nearly a decade, then it was used for storage. Nearly demolished to make way for a park in the 1990s, it is now listed as an historic building. Across the road from the printing house is a row of shophouses, where Phra Sumen Road curves into Phra Athit Road. These were built around 1920 and are rare

Bang Lamphoo

Rama IX sala,
Santi Chai Prakan Park

survivors in the city. Some of them have recently been converted into bars and restaurants and, along with another row further down the street (built in the 1940s and not so decorative), was part of the reason this part of Bang Lamphoo took off around 2000 as one of the best places to go out in the city, even earning the nickname of Bangkok's Left Bank. Across Phra Athit Road from the shophouses sits **Phra Sumen Fort**, one of only two fortifications remaining of the fourteen along Bangkok's old city wall. This hexagonal structure was built by Rama I in 1783 and renovated in 1999 when it was incorporated into **Santi Chai Prakan Park** in honour of the Rama IX's 72nd birthday. The fort sits at the northern end of the new park. Originally the site of a sugar mill, it is now home to a new but traditional-looking Thai-style sala and some lovely landscaped walkways, including a riverfront one that links to nearby Phra Pin Klao Bridge.

Further down Phra Athit Road (at number 102) is **Baan Phra Athit**. Built for a prince around 1925 it is in an eclectic mix of Western styles, mainly Italian with Arts and Crafts notes. Two separate structures are linked via a loggia while the pointy-roofed tower gives the whole ensemble a jaunty air. It was home to the Goethe Institute for many years and is now a restaurant, so it is possible to see part of this charming building if you dine here.

Santi Chai Prakan Park
Opening times: 5am to 10pm daily
Admission: free

Link to the Dusit District walk:
Retrace your steps up Phra Athit and Phra Sumen Roads and turn left onto Samsen Road and walk to the junction with Wisut Kasat Road (which is under the Rama VIII Road flyover). Turn right and Wat Indrawihan will be on your left.

Dusit District

Nearest Chao Phraya Express Pier: Wisut Kasat
Approximate walking time: 2 hours

New Royal City

The Dusit district is the centre of Thai government and is perhaps the only part of Bangkok to retain some of the charm and character of the city prior to the rampant development of the second half of the twentieth century. It still remains Bangkok's royal enclave, home to the royal temple of Wat Benjamabopit (the Marble Temple) and the Chitrlada Palace, the royal family's residence. Political power is also concentrated in Dusit – the National Assembly, Government House, numerous ministries and the prime minister's residence are all located here. It also has its more down-to-earth aspects, with horse-racing at the Royal Turf Club, and Muay Thai boxing at Ratchdamnoen Stadium. It even has a zoo.

THE WALK

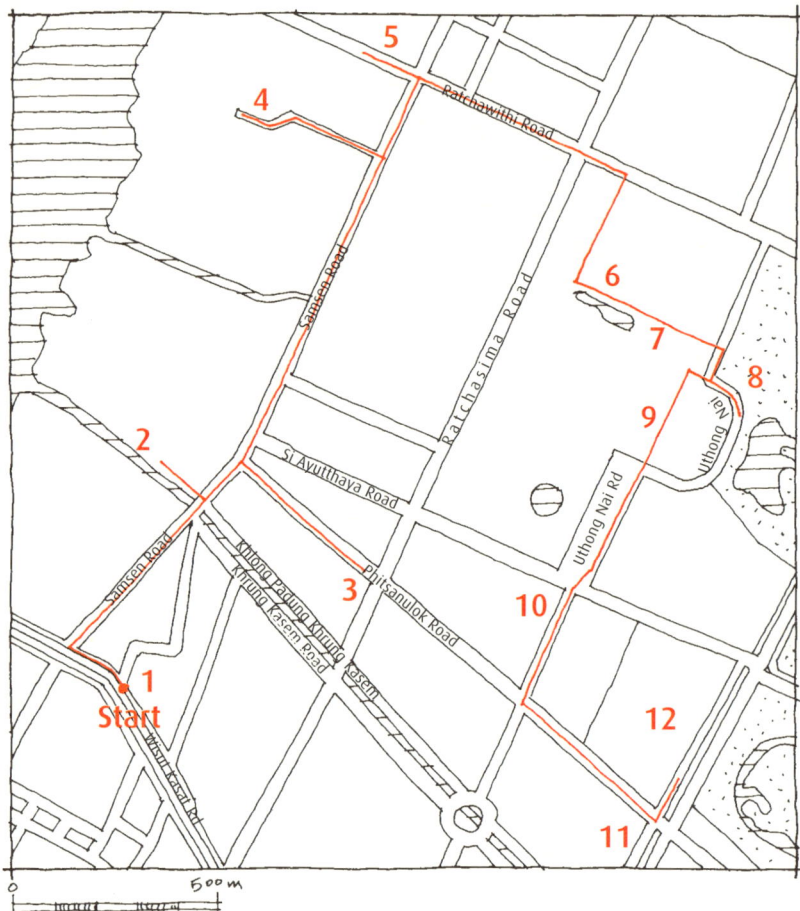

KEY

1. Wat Indrawihan
2. Thewet Flower Market
3. Crown Property Bureau
4. St Francis Xavier Church
5. Dusit Samoson
6. Vimarnmek Palace
7. Abhisek Dusit Throne Hall
8. Dusit Zoo
9. Ananta Samakorn Throne Hall
10. Wang Parusakawan
11. Government House
12. Wat Benjamabophit

Dusit District

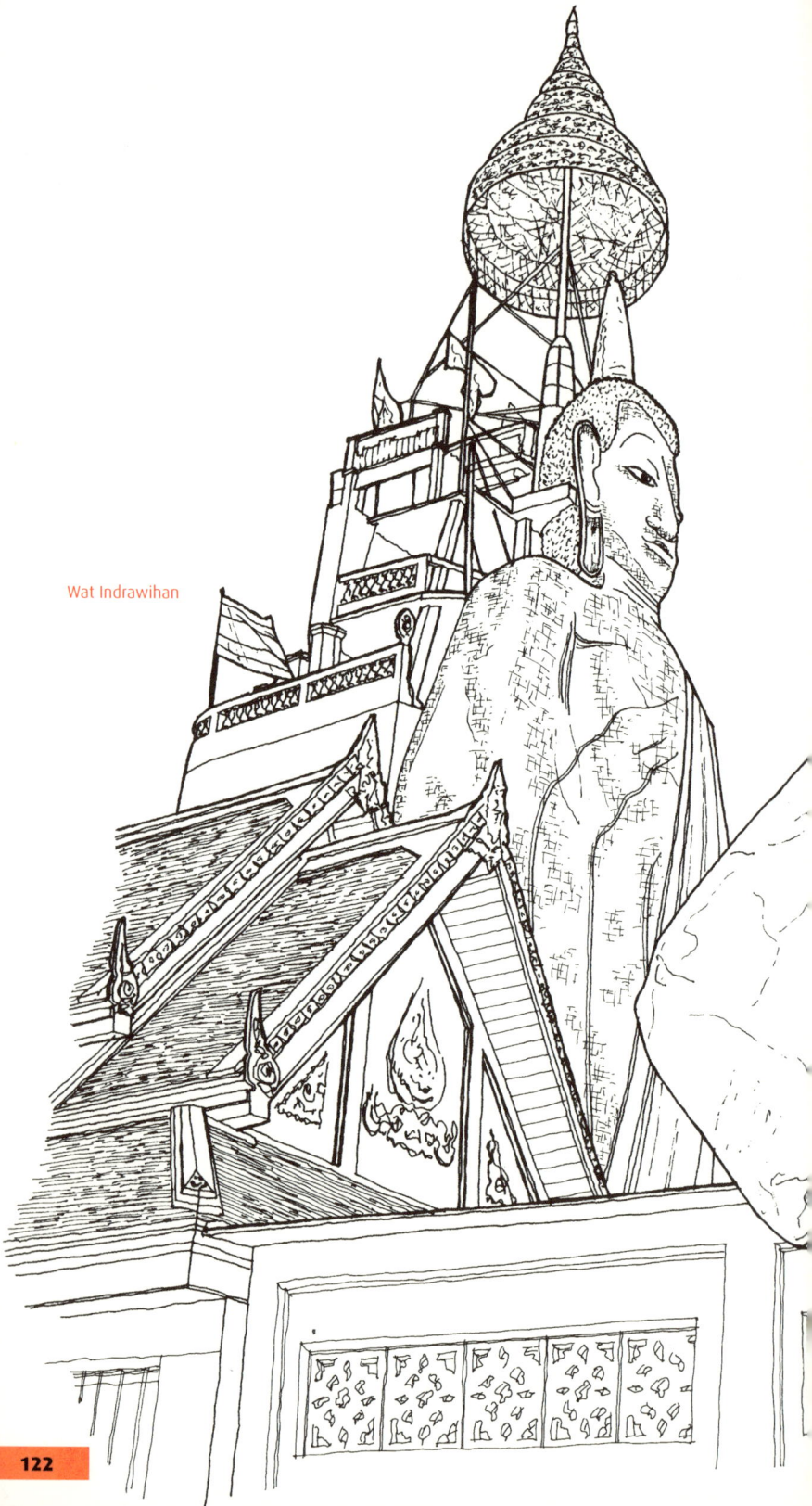

Wat Indrawihan

Wat Indrawihan

If you are walking from the Wisut Kasat Chao Phraya Express Pier, follow Wisut Kasat Road and Wat Indrawihan will be on your left after the junction with Samsen Road. The reason for Wat Indrawihan's claim to fame is not hard to miss: a 32-metre statue of the Buddha (hence its name in English, the Temple of the Standing Buddha). The statue was commissioned in the mid-19th century by Rama IV to house a relic of the Buddha which came from Sri Lanka but it wasn't completed until 1927, about 60 years later. The body is covered in golden mosaic tiles and the face is gold leaf. Relics such as fragments of bone and hair are housed in numerous Buddhist monuments worldwide. This particular standing Buddha could not be considered one of the most beautiful, but it certainly is impressive. Its enormous toes have become an altar for offerings, usually consisting of garlands of fresh flowers. The bot contains hundreds of Benjarong funerary urns, as well as traditional-looking but modern murals. The temple itself dates from the Ayutthaya period but was rebuilt by Rama I for settlers from Laos.

Thewet Flower Market

Retrace your steps back to Samsen Road, turn right and follow it until you come to Khlong Padung Krung Kasem, cross the bridge and the Thewet Flower Market will be on your left down the canal. Located in a sedate corner of this quiet backwater of the city, the Thewet Flower Market is one of Bangkok's premier plant markets and garden centres, offering a colourful array of flowers and plants from all over the country. Flanking both sides of Khlong Phadung

BRACKEN MAY '01

Krung Kasem, it runs west from Samsen Road to the Chao Phyra River and as well as plants stocks an enormous range of gardening goods, including ornamental pots, pond bases and other items. Although Thewet Market is not as extensive as Chatuchak Market, its prices are generally lower and it is a pleasant place to browse because not so busy.

Thewet Flower Market
Opening times: 9:30am to 7:30pm daily
Admission: free

Crown Property Bureau
Return to Samsen Road and turn left, then take a right onto Phitsanulok Road. The Crown Property Bureau is housed in the old Ladawan Palace on the corner of Ratchasima Road. This lovely, large neoclassical building was built for one of Rama V's children around 1908 and is also known as Wang Daeng (Red Palace) because of the colour of the compound's original walls. The palace itself is painted an attractive mix of yellow and white and had some finely executed decorative plasterwork between the windows. The main block is two-storey and symmetrical but this is linked to a large and asymmetrical three-storey wing which sports a tall octagonal turret. Occupied by the Japanese during World War II, it was used briefly as a base by the Allies before being bought by the Crown Property Bureau — the body established in 1936 to oversee a portfolio of heritage buildings.

Martin de Castro building,
St Gabriel's College

St Francis Xavier Church

Retrace your steps to Samsen Road and turn right and you will come to the **National Library** on your left after the junction with Si Ayutthaya Road. Founded when Rama V amalgamated three of the Grand Palace's royal libraries in 1905, it moved to a site near Wat Mahatat in 1916. This building, which also houses the National Archives, was built in the mid-1960s and incorporates several traditional Thai architectural touches (as do many of the government offices in this part of the city, enlivening otherwise bland modern buildings). The lobby contains a number of paintings by well-known Thai artists, while the library itself contains a large collection of books in both Thai and English.

Continue along Samsen Road and you will see **St Gabriel's College** on your left. This is a Catholic boys' school established in 1920 and housed in an attractive cluster of buildings, including the Italianate three-storey Martin de Castro building built by a French architect in 1922 and, to the left, the seven-storey De Montfort Hall, which is by a local firm and one of the best examples of 1960s architecture in the city.

On the left just past St Gabriel's College is Soi Samsen 11. Follow this soi as it winds its way through a small enclave of Christian churches and schools that runs all the way to the banks of the Chao Phraya River. The **St Francis Xavier Church** is perhaps the most striking of these buildings, with its portico of three tall arches facing towards the river. It is named after the Jesuit priest who travelled to Asia to try and spread Christianity. Land was granted by Rama III and a small bamboo church was built. This was replaced in the 1860s by this simple neoclassical building which has a statue of St Francis over its rear pediment. The church was restored in 2010.

Dusit Samoson

Dusit Samoson

Return to Samsen Road and turn left. Then take a left onto Ratchawithi Road and the Dusit Samoson will be on your right a little way down the road. This Arts and Crafts-style residence dating from around 1910 is part of an upmarket apartment complex. Originally it was a private residence and is a rare example of a large and comfortable home built for a private Thai citizen, as opposed to all the homes for princes and wealthy foreigners that survive throughout the rest of the city.

Vimarnmek Palace

Retrace your steps up Ratchawithi Road, cross Samsen Road and keep going until you reach **Dusit Park** on your right. Also known as the Celestial Garden, Dusit Park was built as a new royal city and was connected to the Grand

Vimarnmek Palace

Suan Hong Residential hall

Palace via Ratchdamnoen Avenue (intended to be a Thai Champs-Elysées). It is still an oasis of calm today with wide, tree-shaded avenues and *khlongs* lined with Edwardian-era mansions, often in an eclectic mix of Western styles. Home to a number of museums, including the **Royal Carriage Museum**, which contains royal vehicles, including vintage cars and ceremonial carriages, and is housed in two mews buildings; the **Old Clock Museum**, which has a small collection of antique timepieces from a variety of countries; the **Royal Family Museum,** with photographs and paintings of members of the Chakri dynasty and **Rama IX's Photographic Museum,** with photographs taken by the current king, a keen amateur photographer.

Undoubtedly the highlight of any visit is **Vimarnmek Palace**. The name means 'palace of angels in the clouds' and it is the world's largest golden teak building (with more than 80 rooms). Constructed without using a single nail (wooden pegs were used instead), this three-storey mansion was originally built on Kho Si Chang in 1892 but moved here in 1901

Dusit District

where it became a favourite retreat of Rama V, who lived here with his family while waiting for the nearby Chitrlada Palace to be built. The king was the only adult male allowed live in the palace and the octagonal tower was his private quarters. The rooms are decorated in Biedermeier style and feature European, Siamese and Chinese ornaments. The palace was the first building in Thailand to have electricity and an indoor bathroom. It closed in 1932 and was used for storage until Queen Sirikit had it restored in time for Bangkok's bicentennial celebrations in 1982. The palace overlooks a small lake known as Jade Pool, onto which an elegant little pavilion protrudes. This affords excellent

Did You Know?

Queen Saovapha, wife of Rama V, kept the same nocturnal hours as her husband and nothing was allowed to disturb her during the day while she slept. All traffic on the road outside was diverted and even birds were kept at bay by guards patrolling the grounds armed with silent weapons like blow pipes.

views of the traditional teak houses Rama V had built around 1904 so that he could live in traditional style when he chose, and also entertain up-country guests in a less formal setting than the palace.

Vimarnmek Palace
Opening times: 9:30am to 4pm daily
Admission charges (which covers Grand Palace as well)

Abhisek Dusit Throne Hall

The Abhisek Dusit Throne Hall is adjacent to the Vimarnmek Palace gardens and is a showcase for the traditional arts and crafts that have were saved from decline by Queen Sirikit, who founded the Promotion of Supplementary Occupations and Related Techniques (SUPPORT). The foundation is housed in a small, intricately decorated building of wood, brick and stucco built in 1904 and somewhat reminiscent of a gingerbread house. Traditional handicrafts on display include nielloware, celadon, lacquerware and an amazing art form that uses the iridescent green-blue wings of jewel beetles. Some of the designs have been created by members of the royal family.

Abhisek Dusit Throne Hall
Opening times: 9:30am to 4pm daily
Admission charges (which covers Grand Palace as well)

Dusit Zoo

Exit the grounds of the Ananta Samakorn Throne Hall via Uthong Nai Road and the **Royal Elephant Museum** will be across the road. This was the old stable building for white elephants — any white elephant found anywhere in the country was automatically the property of the king. The displays here include information about how to capture and train elephants and includes some of the implements their handlers (mahouts) use. Farther along Uthong Nai Road, just at the corner where it veers to the right, is the entrance to **Dusit Zoo**. These lush grounds were originally a private botanical garden for Rama V and some varieties of tropical flora are still cultivated here. It sits at the heart of a green belt which runs from Dusit Park to the Chitrlada Palace. Turned into a public zoo in 1938, it is one of Asia's best and has good provision of space for its birds and larger mammals and thanks to its tropical location the elephants are in their native habitat. The zoo contains a number of lawns, woods and lakes, which are pleasant for strolling in, as well as a charming **Glass House** which overlooks the lake. Built around 1920, this single-storey steel-frame wooden building was a reception hall for the royal family and is now the director's office.

Royal Elephant Museum
Opening times: 9:30am to 4pm daily
Admission charges (which covers Grand Palace as well)

Dusit Zoo
Opening times: 8am to 6pm daily
Admission charges

Note: White Elephants
The white elephant (chang samkhan) has been important in Thailand since the days when Buddha walked the earth. It is said that Queen Maya became pregnant with the future Buddha after dreaming of a white elephant entered her womb. Ever since the thirteenth century, when King Ramkamhaeng of Sukhothai gave the animal great prestige, the reigning king's status is reputed to depend on the number of white elephants he owns. It has also served as the national icon, being a part of the Siamese flag until 1917. The origin of the phrase 'white elephant', meaning something useless and expensive, comes from the tradition of the Thai king presenting his enemies with one or more of these beasts; expensive to maintain, yet forbidden to put them to work, they tended to take the recipient's mind off troublemaking.

Ananta Samakorn Throne Hall and the King Rama V Equestrian Statue

Ananta Samakorn Throne Hall

Return to Uthong Nai Road after leaving Dusit Zoo you will see the Ananta Samakorn Throne Hall straight ahead of you to the left. This vast, ornate, Italianate throne hall was built in between 1907 and 1916 and was, for a time, home to the Thai parliament. It is still occasionally used for royal receptions and private functions. It has a spectacular interior based on St Peter's in Rome and has, since 1992, showcased arts and crafts from the Queen Sirikit institute. The throne hall also acts as the focal point at the end of Ratchdamnoen Avenue, which runs all the way to Sanam Luang. The impressive bronze **Rama V equestrian statue** at the centre of the parade ground in front of the throne hall from 1908 and was cast in Paris. It is the focus of a memorial held each year on 23 October, the anniversary of Rama V's death, when the square is crowded with Thais honouring the memory of the dead king by laying wreaths at the base of the statue. The parade ground is also the site of Thailand's annual Trooping of the Colours ceremony every December.

Ananta Samakorn Throne Hall
Opening times: 8:30am to 4:30pm daily
Admission charges (which covers Grand Palace as well)

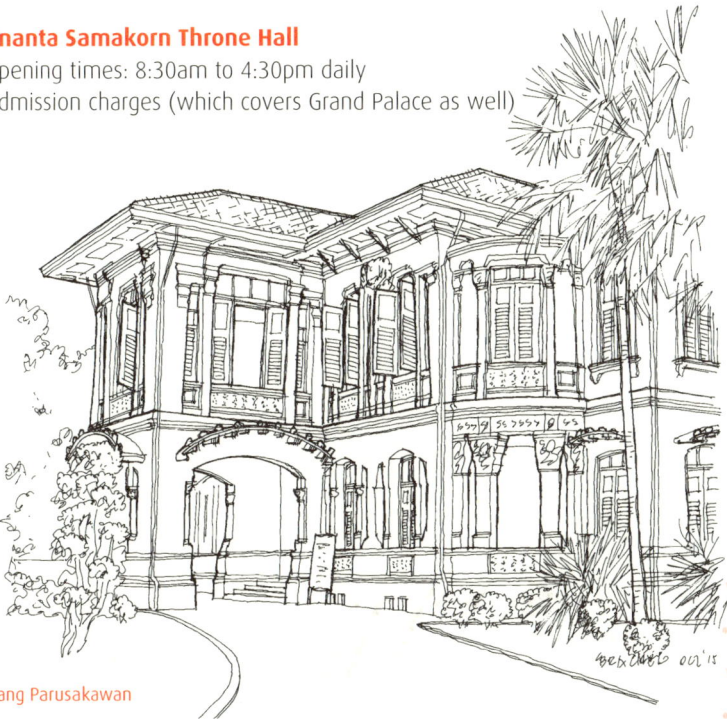

Wang Parusakawan

> **Did You Know?**
> Rama V introduced chairs into the kingdom: before his reign, Thais sat on the floor, or on floor cushions.

Wang Parusakawan

Continue past the Rama V equestrian statue, cross Si Auytthaya Road and you will see Wang Parusakawan on the corner of Ratchdamnoen Avenue on your right. Actually this complex comprises two large villas, both with royal connections. The first one, actually known as **Villa Chitralada**, is a gorgeous two-storey mansion with a porte-cochere sitting at an angle across its prominent site. It was a gift to Rama VI from his father but when he became king he gave it to another of his brothers. Built around 1903, it is a long low building in a German Art Nouveau style. It was converted into offices in 1932 and is in excellent condition. Painted yellow and white, like so many of the villas in this district, its shutters, being green, mark a pleasant and subtle contrast. Next door to the Villa Chitralada farther along this stretch of Ratchdamnoen Avenue is **Wang Parusakawan**, another beautiful mansion and also a gift from Rama V to one his sons, Prince Chakrabongse, after he returned from a stint in the military academy of St Petersburg. A larger and more rambling mansion than its neighbour, it dates from around 1906 and is an altogether more romantic looking building. The National Police Department moved into the compound in 1952 and the Villa Chitralada was for a time a police museum. Some buildings were added to the compound in the 1960s and were recently given a sleek makeover. These glass boxes, dating from 2012, sit in the beautifully landscaped grounds between the two villas.

Government House

Government House

Continue down Ratchdamnoen Avenue and turn left onto Phitsanulok Road and you will come to Government House on your right overlooking the Prem Prachakon canal. This remarkable building, in a dazzling Venetian-gothic idiom, was built by Rama VI in 1926 for one of his aides-de-camp (he also built another Venetian fantasy on nearby Phitsanulok Road for another aide around the same time). Superbly detailed, it makes reference to such Venetian landmarks as the Doge's Palace, St Mark's Cathedral and the Ca' d'Oro on the Grand Canal. Originally called Villa Norasingh (and also known as the Thai Khu Fa Building), it was bought by the government in 1941 to prevent it being used by the Japanese as an embassy. Its lavish interiors now host state functions as well as prime minister's cabinet meetings.

Wat Benjamabophit

Turn left up Nakhon Pathom Road and Wat Benjamabophit will be on your left. This large compound is home not only to the famous temple but also to the

Wat Benjamabophit School, which was founded by Rama V in 1900. The large pink symmetrical neoclassical building dates from 1902 and is in a Renaissance style with some baroque flourishes (such as the split pediment over the entrance block). **Wat Benjamabophit** itself, which is also known as the Marble Temple, is an extremely successful hybrid of Thai and European architectural elements. It is not old, having been begun by Rama V in 1900 (in fact Wat Benjamabophit means 'temple of the fifth king'). The king commissioned his brother, Prince Naris, an architect, to supervise the project which was designed by two Italian architects, Carlo Allegri and Mario Tamagno. They designed a new bot and cloister that made lavish use of Carrera marble (hence the name). Laid out in a cruciform style with traditional Thai cascading roofs, the bot is elegantly proportioned, it also contains another successful fusing of different traditions with stained-glass windows made in Florence in the 1950s depicting scenes from Thai mythology. The Thai atmosphere is further reinforced by the use of yellow as the predominant colour. The temple is well-known for three sets of beautiful doors inlaid with mother-of-pearl salvaged from Wat Borom Buddharam in Ayutthaya. The room housing the ashes of Rama V also contains the revered copy of Phitsanulok's Phra Buddha Chinarat, which is distinguished by a pointed halo. While the building, which was Rama V's home when he was a monk, features murals depicting events that occurred during his reign. Ranged around the cloister are 53 different Buddha images, both originals and copies from Thailand and other Buddhist countries, which the king assembled. The wat is a popular location for witnessing Buddhist monastic rituals, especially the daily alms round, in which people looking to make merit donate food to the monks who line up along Nakhon Pathom Road, the exact opposite of the usual practice, where monks go out in search of alms.

Wat Benjamabophit
Opening times: 8:30am to 4:30pm daily
Admission charges

End of walks

Canal, Wat Benjamabophit

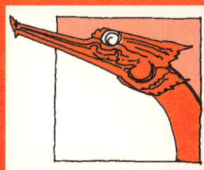

Further Afield

Other places of interest within easy reach of the city centre

Further Afield

This chapter covers individual but isolated architectural gems, such as the Suan Pakkad Palace and the Siam Society compound, as well as Chulalongkorn University. It also deals with interesting and historic buildings not covered on previous walks, such as Wat Arun and the Royal Barge Museum. It also gives a brief guide to Thailand's most famous market, the Chatuchak Weekend Market.

GREATER BANGKOK

0   2.5 km

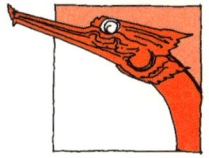

KEY

1. Wat Arun
2. Royal Barge Museum
3. Chulalongkorn University
4. Siam Society
5. Suan Pakkad Palace
6. Chatuchak Weekend Market

Further Afield

Wat Arun

The nearest Chao Phraya Express Pier to the temple is Thien, you can then get a ferry across the river. Wat Arun, also known as the Temple of the Dawn, is one of the most striking edifices in Bangkok and a city landmark. It is ancient and has had a number of name changes, being known previously as Wat Makok and Wat Cheng before being named in honour of Aruna, the Indian god of the dawn. It is said that in October 1767 King Taksin arrived here at sunrise from the sacked capital, Ayutthaya, and decided that this would be the new home of the Emerald Buddha, he then set about enlarging what was quite a small temple into a royal chapel. Rama I and II were mainly responsible for the size of the current temple while in the 19th century Rama IV added the ornamentation which depicts flowers said to evoke the vegetation of Mount Meru, the mythical home of the gods. This decoration, consisting of numerous pieces of broken porcelain donated by local people, is one of the temple's most unusual and attractive features. Up close it looks odd, but from a distance it achieves an eye-catching and colourful effect, especially when seen glittering in the low sunlight of both dawn and dusk. Seen from the river, as it was ideally meant to be viewed, the temple's striking silhouette is impressive. The monument's style, more akin to Khmer architecture than anything else, is unique in Thailand and is the logo of the Tourism Authority of Thailand.

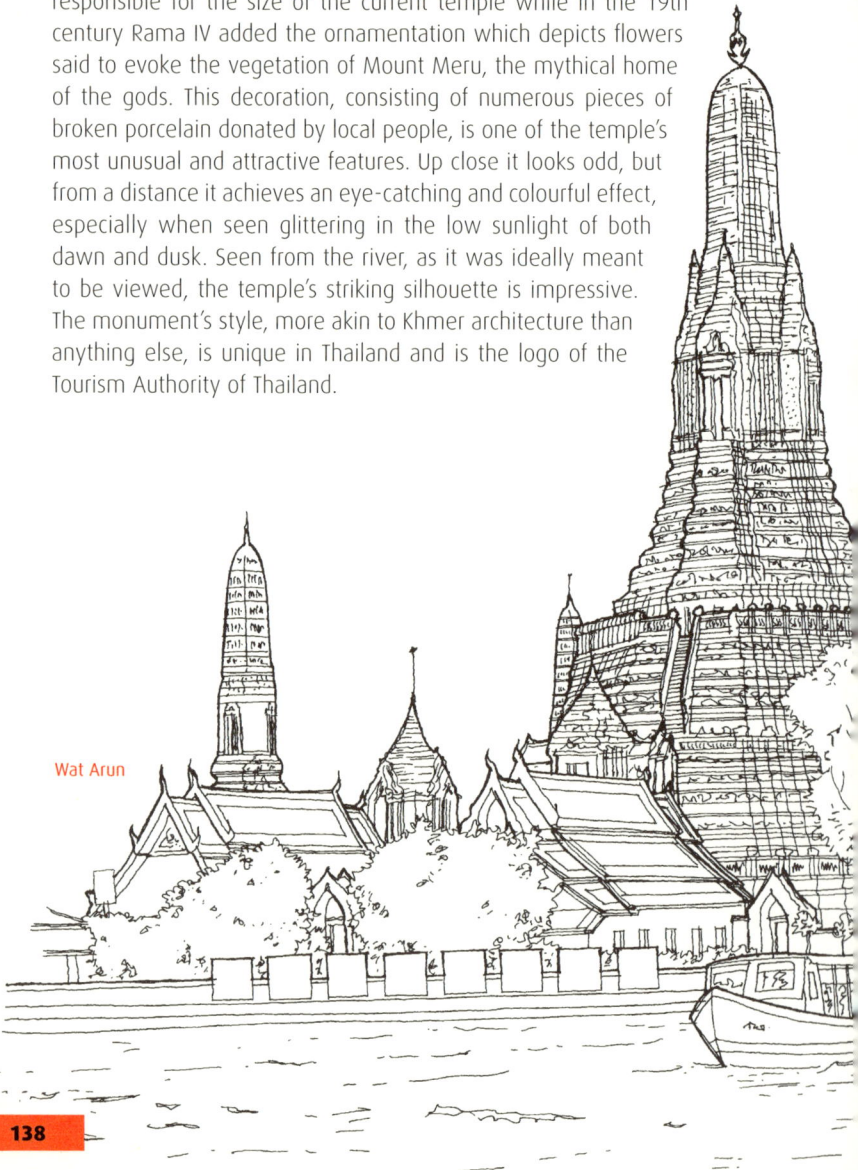

Wat Arun

The monument's design symbolises Hindu-Buddhist cosmology, with the 67-metre-high central *prang* supposed to represent mythical Mount Meru and its ornamental tiers being worlds within worlds. The quincunx layout of the four minor *prangs* around the central one is a symbolic mandala shape (in Sanskrit the circular figure is seen as a religious symbol of the universe). The circumference of the base is 234 metres, with mondops located at the cardinal points. The rest of the temple complex contains buildings typically found in a Thai *wat*, with the image of the Buddha in the main *bot* sitting above the ashes of devotees. There are a number of Chinese guard figures located at the entrance to the terrace, and these nicely compliment the Chinese-style porcelain decorating the *prangs*.

Wat Arun
Opening times: 8:30am to 5:30pm daily
Admission charges

Did You Know?
This temple was originally known as Wat Cheng but when King Taksin passed it at dawn one morning in 1767 and saw how run-down it had become he vowed to have it restored. It was renamed Wat Arun (Temple of the Dawn) as a result.

BRACKEN AUG '01

Royal Barge Museum

The nearest Chao Phraya Express Pier to this museum is Phra Pinklao. The kingdom's royal barges, a number of which are still used for special occasions such as auspicious royal birthdays, are housed in this warehouse-like structure which became a museum in 1974. Apart from the decorative boats, the museum also contains a number of ceremonial objects used in river processions, as well as an exhibition showing the evolution of these processions and ship-building methods past and present. Most of the boats in the royal collection are reproductions of those built by Rama I, some others are kept at Wasukree Pier, with more in the Small Boats Section of the Royal Navy. Suphanahong (Golden Swan) is the most important barge in the collection, made during the reign of Rama VI from a single piece of teak more than 50 metres long, it weighs 15 tonnes. Anantanagaraj, bearing a multi-headed naga, is reserved for conveying important Buddha images.

Royal Barge Museum
Opening times: 9am to 5pm daily
Admission charges

Note: Royal Transport

The Khanham was a covered sedan chair used by the king or females of the royal family and sometimes also by high-ranking aristocrats during the era of Thailand's absolute monarchy. Sedan chairs, or palanquins, were used for official ceremonies as well as informal visits from the Ayutthaya to the Rattanakosin periods. There were four different types: the Yannamat was used by the king during royal ceremonies, while the roofless Saliang served for more general occasions. The Wo, which resembled the Saliang except for its canopy, and Khanham, with its single pole supporting a cradle at its centre, were preferred for long journeys.

Chulalongkorn University

The nearest Skytrain station is National Stadium. Leave via Rama I Road in the direction of Phayathai Road. Turn right down Phayathai Road and Chulalongkorn University takes up most of the left-hand side of the road after

Chulalongkorn University

Soi Chulalongkorn 62. Enter the campus by the gates overlooking the park and lake. Founded in 1916 by Rama VI, and named in honour of his father King Chulalongkorn (Rama V), Thailand's oldest and most prestigious university covers two blocks of the city's downtown. The university's central gardens, between Phyathai and Henri Dunant Roads, are the site of several attractive buildings, many of which are in the Rattanakosin style, an attractive hybrid of Thai and Western architecture, and there is a large lake which is often used during the Loy Krathong festival. Home to a number of museums and galleries, the university also contains an auditorium, which is mainly used for classical concerts. It is a pleasant place to stroll in, especially during term time when the neatly uniformed students can be seen milling around the grounds.

Siam Society

Asoke is the nearest Skytrain station. Leave it and follow Sukhumvit Road, turning left onto Soi Asoke (Soi Sukhumvit 21) and the Siam Society will be on your left. This foundation is under royal patronage and was established in 1904 to promote the study of Thai history, botany, zoology, anthropology and linguistics. It publishes a scholarly journal containing articles by experts on these subjects and is also home to an excellent reference library. The society's headquarters shares its compound with two interesting buildings, the first of these, **Kamthieng House**, is a traditional Lanna-style house from Chiang Mai and dates from the 1840s. It was moved here in the 1960s and differs from other Thai houses in the city (e.g. the Suan Pakkad Palace or Jim Thompson's

Further Afield

141

House) not only because of the style but also because it was the home of an ordinary Thai person, not royalty. The objects on display in the house give an idea of what life was like in northern Thailand in the mid-nineteenth century. The furniture is sparse, with only a couple of low tables and seating mats arranged across the polished wooden floors. Surplus furniture and utensils are stored in the rafters. The veranda connecting the kitchen to the granary overlooks a garden which has been made to look as authentic as possible. Nestling close to Kamthieng House is the more recently acquired **Sangaroon House**. A traditional Ayutthaya-style house built in 1988 to house a collection of folk craftwork. The fascinating display includes baskets, fishing pots and takraw balls.

Siam Society

Opening times: 9am to 5pm, Tue-Sat
Admission charges

Sangaroon House

Suan Pakkad Palace

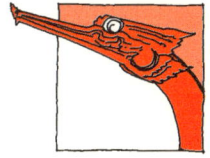

The nearest Skytrain station is Phayathai. Leaving it, follow Phayathai Road and turn right onto Si Ayutthaya Road and the Suan Pakkad Palace will be on your right. This palace was the home of Prince and Princess Chumbhot. It consists of a cluster of eight traditional teak houses assembled in the 1950s on land that was originally a cabbage patch ('suan pakkad' in Thai, hence its rather odd-sounding English name 'cabbage patch palace'). Princess Chumbhot was an avid gardener and created the lush landscaped garden we see today. Both she and her husband were also avid art collectors and the palace has been converted into a museum to house their impressive private collections of art and artefacts. Their tastes were wide-ranging, resulting in an eclectic selection of objects from antique lacquered furniture, to Khmer sculpture, and even includes a selection of traditional Thai musical instruments. There is also an important collection of whorl-patterned red-and-white Bronze Age pottery, excavated from tombs at Ban Chiang in Northeast Thailand. The highlight of any visit simply has to be the exquisite Lacquer Pavilion which was built from two temple buildings retrieved by Prince Chumbhot from Ayutthaya province. Immaculately crafted, the pavilion's interior contains beautifully detailed black-and-gold lacquered murals depicting scenes from Buddha's life and the Ramakien. They also, even more interestingly, portray ordinary Thai life up to the fall of Ayutthaya in 1767.

Suan Pakkad Palace

Further Afield

Scenes include foreigners trading goods, traditional Thai markets, graphic battle scenes and there are even some vivid depictions of the Thai version of hell. These murals are some of the very few to survive intact from the Ayutthaya period.

Suan Pakkad Palace
Opening times: 9am to 4pm daily
Admission charges

Chatuchak Weekend Market

Located right beside Kamphaeng Phet MRT station, this extremely popular and very traditional weekend market started life on Sanam Luang. It eventually outgrew its position and moved to Chatuchak Park in 1982, where it was initially considered to be too far out of the city, but as Bangkok has spread the market has become something of a centre in its own right. Bangkok's biggest weekend market, it is said to cover the size of five football fields and is home to more than 6,000 stalls with a bewildering array of goods on offer, ranging from antiques to discount designer clothes and accessories. There is even a hill-tribe section selling artefacts and textiles from all over Thailand and some neighbouring countries. There is a plant section with every conceivable specimen of Thai flora, while the food stalls offer a huge range of fresh farm produce and seafood. Always thronged with people, bargain hunters and window shoppers alike, it is a pleasant and interesting place to spend a weekend afternoon.

Chatuchak Weekend Market
Opening times: 7am to 6pm, Sat–Sun
Admission: free

Chatuchak Weekend Market

Architectural Styles

This chapter explains some of the architectural styles mentioned in the book. Beginning with the different traditional house styles to be found in various parts of Thailand it then outlines the five main historic periods of Thai architecture, from Khmer to Rattanakosin. There are also notes on Western architectural styles, such as neoclassical and gothic, as well as an overview of the various forms and styles of the different places of worship to be found in the city, including Buddhist, Chinese and Indian temples as well as Muslim mosques and Christian churches.

Traditional Thai House

Traditional Thai houses are well adapted to the tropical climate, using natural materials such as hardwoods, bamboo and dried leaves. They are raised on stilts to protect them from flooding and have steeply slanted roofs the better to throw off rainwater.

Central Plains House

The central plains are the hottest part of the country and a large veranda is common. Acting as an outside living area, it sometimes has several houses clustered around it.

Water House

Houses built on water are common in flood-prone Bangkok and along the rivers of the central plains. They are either built on posts above the water line or on bamboo rafts which float during floods.

Shophouse

Shophouses used to be a common building type in Bangkok, as they were throughout Asia. The family usually lives above the business premises, which can be anything from a small workshop to a shop or restaurant. Usually two- to three-storeys in height, the neoclassical style predominates. There are also some handsome Art Deco examples dating from the 1920s onwards, and in Chinatown there are some unusual gothic-style ones.

Spirit House

These can be seen everywhere in Bangkok. Small structures, usually on poles, built to placate the spirits of the land — and when you see a patch of virgin forest in Thailand you can understand the Thais' reverence for the spirit of so mysterious a place. These little houses are the first thing built when land is cleared and are adorned daily with offerings of incense, food and flowers.

Spirit House

Thai Architectural Styles

Khmer

9th to 13th Centuries

Temple complexes, mostly made of stone, were built by the Khmers in northeast Thailand and usually contained staircases lined with carved *nagas* leading to a central sanctuary, often decorated with reliefs depicting Hindu myths, and topped by a central *prang*. Wat Arun (Temple of the Dawn) on the Chao Phraya River is a Khmer-style temple.

Sukhothai

Mid-13th to 15th Centuries

Thailand's 14th-century capital saw the most radical leap in the country's architecture. King Si Intharathit and his successors built *wihans* and *bots* to house images of the Buddha amid the ruins of earlier Khmer structures. *Chedis*, modelled on the bell-shaped reliquary towers of Sri Lanka, were often added. The Sukhothai Hotel on Sathorn Road borrows elegantly from this architectural tradition.

Ayutthaya

Mid-14th to 18th Centuries

Little of the architecture of Ayutthaya survived the destruction of the Burmese invasion of 1767 but the style seems to have been a subtle modification of Khmer *prangs* and Sri Lankan-style *chedis*, with elaborate decoration of *cho fas* and door and window pediments. Wat Ratchaburana in Chinatown has an Ayutthaya-style *prang*.

Lanna

Mid-13th to 19th Centuries

The religious buildings from this period took their influence from Sukhothai, India and Sri Lanka. Although few buildings remain from Lanna's golden age of the 14th and 15th centuries, later temples, in places like Chiang Mai, often featured the intricate woodcarving and gilded *cho fas* and murals associated with this style. The small Wat Muang Kae on Charoen Krung Soi 36 has Lanna-style decorative features.

Lanna style (Wat Muang Kae)

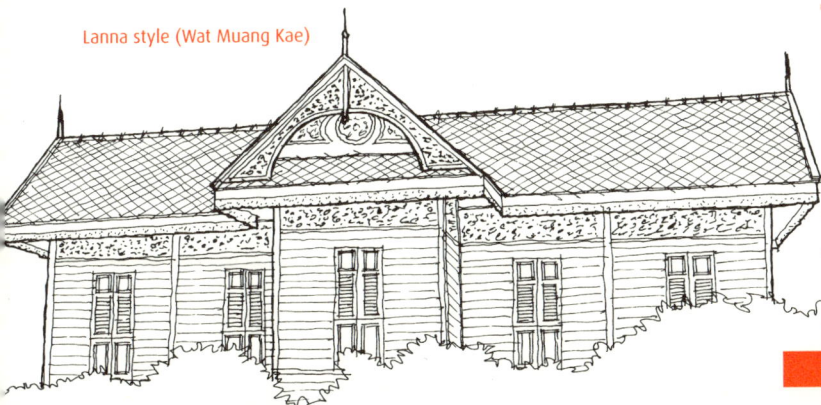

Rattanakosin style (arch, Grand Palace)

Rattanakosin
Late 18th Century to present day
Also known as the Bangkok style, the first *wihans* and *bots* built in the new capital after the fall of Auytthaya were similar to the ones that had been destroyed by the Burmese. Later, larger and more elaborate temples were built, while by the end of the 19th century buildings such as Wat Benjamabophit (Marble Temple) increasingly borrowed from the West, as did many of the buildings in the Grand Palace complex. The balcony in the Grand Palace complex overlooking Sanam Chai Road is typically Rattanakosin in style with a mix of Thai and Western elements.

Western Architectural Styles
Neoclassical
While the shiny new skyscrapers and endless vistas of dusty concrete apartment blocks do tend to give some of downtown Bangkok a somewhat Western flavour they hardly do much to advertise the elegance of the West's architectural achievements. There are, however, some rather more attractive imports to be found in the city. These invariably fall into one of two styles: neoclassical or gothic. Neoclassicism was a throwback to ancient Greece and Rome. This style was elegant and harmonious but disappeared with the fall of the Roman Empire. It was revived in the 17th century, first in Italy and then throughout the rest of Europe and North America, thanks to Andrea Palladio, an Italian architect who studied the ruins of ancient Rome and adapted their styles to suit his era. With the spread of the European empires the style became global.

Neoclassical outbuilding, Baan Manangkhasila (Lan Luang Road)

Architectural Styles

Gothic

This style developed in Northern Europe in the 12th century. Its most distinguishing characteristic is the pointed arch. The gothic style died out by the Renaissance but experienced a revival in the 19th century. A battle raged between gothic and neoclassical style throughout the 19th century in Europe, although the gothic never really caught on in a big way in Asia.

Places of Worship
Thai Temples

The tolerant nature of the Thai people means that there are many places of worship in the city belonging to other faiths. Thai temples dominate, however. These are Buddhist and are built along guidelines that have changed little over the centuries. Invariably they are elaborately decorated, they also have a very practical function, acting as a sort of community centre, particularly in rural areas. Home to monks or nuns, rarely will there be a temple without a monastery attached to it. Laid out with

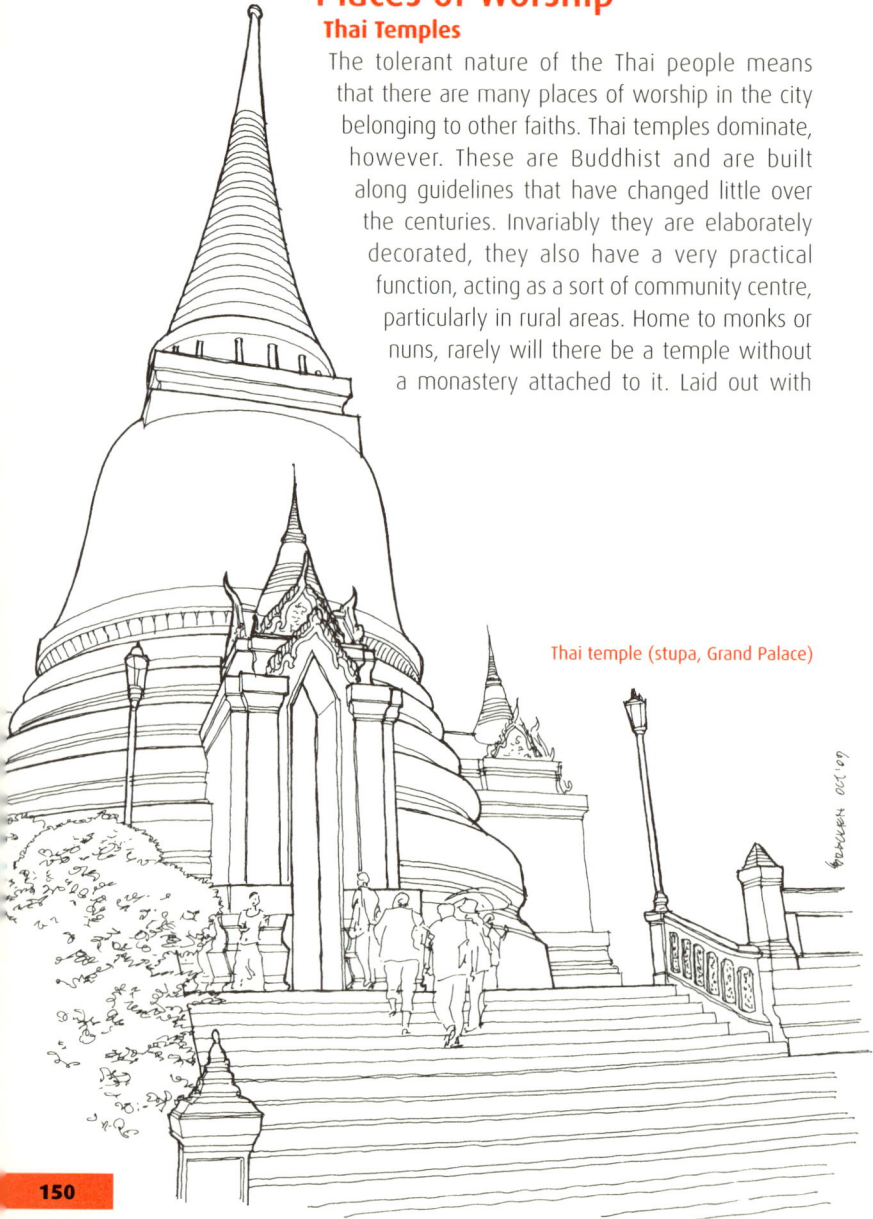

Thai temple (stupa, Grand Palace)

particular care to religious symbolism, the typical elements of a Buddhist temple are the bodhi tree, usually found only in larger temples — the Buddha is supposed to have sat underneath one of these trees while attempting to achieve Enlightenment. The *bot* is an ordination hall, usually reserved for monks, it faces east and is often home to the temple's most important image of the Buddha. A *chedi* is a solid structure, usually bell-shaped, encasing a relic of the Buddha or the ashes of a king, a number of temples were specifically built around a sacred *chedi*. The cloister encloses the main part of the temple and its walls are often decorated with murals, in more important temples statues of the Buddha are housed here in rows. Usually only the larger temples will have a library of sacred texts, and these are housed in a building known as the *ho tri*. A *mondop* is a square-based structure, usually containing an object of veneration, topped with a spire, while the *wihan* is an assembly hall, similar to the *bot*, but usually larger and accessible by the laity, there may be more than one in a temple complex.

Chinese Temples

The form of the traditional Chinese temple is usually based on that of the traditional Chinese house, consisting of a group of pavilions ranged around open courtyards. They are also usually built in strict accordance with the precepts of feng shui in an attempt to achieve a balance between the temple's Yin and Yang elements. Location also plays an important part in the decision to construct a Chinese temple — situating them close to water

Chinese temple (Da Ben Tou Gong Temple, Songwat Road)

will lend them favourable feng shui. Usually dedicated to one specific deity, Chinese temples can also be dedicated to more than one god, some are even syncretic, which means that any number of different Chinese faiths (Buddhist, Taoist, Confucian, etc.,) are welcome to worship there. They are invariably rich in gilt-covered decorative carvings, mouldings and murals, often with the dragon as a prominent decorative feature.

Indian Temples

Bangkok has a number of important Hindu temples. Elaborately sculpted, they stand out even in this garish city. Always square in plan (Hindus regard the square as the perfect shape), a complex set of rules governs the siting, design and building of each temple. These rules are based on numerology, astronomy, astrology and religious law and are so complicated that it's customary for each temple to keep its own set of calculations, almost as if they were religious texts. Each temple is dedicated to a particular god. Temples are a constant hub of activity and a focal point for the Hindu community, who gather to celebrate many different rites and festivals. Many Thais also worship in Hindu temples because the Buddhist faith sprang directly from Hinduism (and Buddha was born in Lumphini, India).

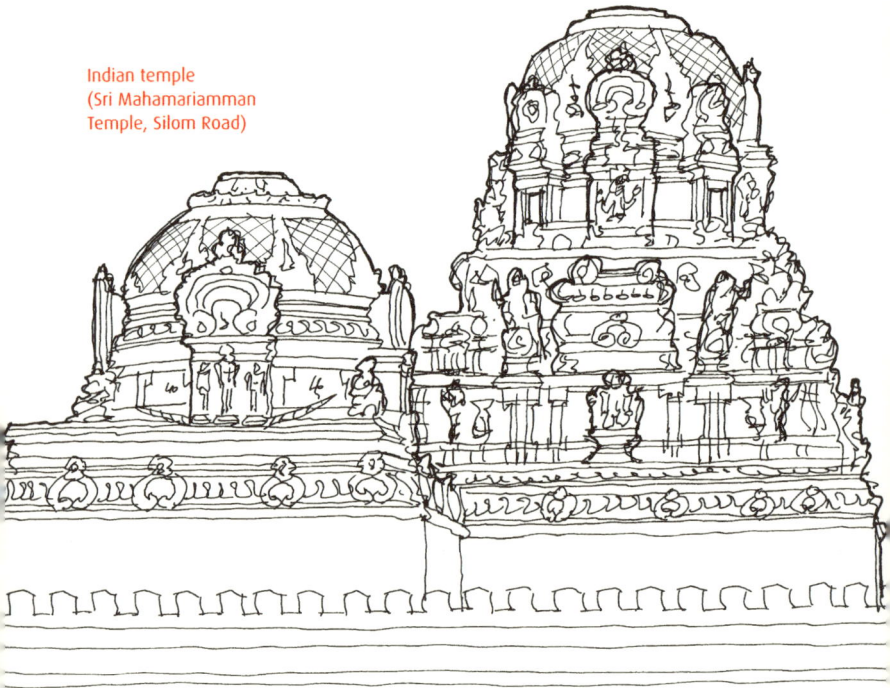

Indian temple
(Sri Mahamariamman
Temple, Silom Road)

Muslim mosque
(Suwannaphum Mosque,
Khlong Wa Thong Phleng)

Muslim Mosques

Arabs from the Middle East traded in Thailand centuries before Bangkok was founded. Thailand's immediate neighbours to the South, Malaysia and Indonesia, are Muslim countries, while a large proportion of the population in southern Thailand is also Muslim, and there are significant pockets of Islamic faith dotted around the capital. Their mosques are traditional in their form and layout, invariable domed, but often have only one minaret, from which the muezzin calls the faithful to prayer. Not as grand or imposing as the mosques typically built by Thailand's neighbours, they often have more charm and character as a result. They also often act as a centre for Islamic studies.

Christian Churches

Bangkok has quite a number of Christian places of worship, these tend to have a standard cross-shaped layout for both Roman Catholic and Protestant churches. By about the 5th century, when the Roman Empire was collapsing, people were converting to Christianity in increasingly larger numbers. To accommodate the crowds, market places, known as basilicas, became used as places of worship, and Christian churches for the next few hundred years tended to follow this form, being rather heavy, square-shaped structures. After 800 AD, and the establishment of the Holy Roman Empire under Charlemagne, western-European Christians became galvanised and this new spirit of identity was reflected in their buildings. Advances in building technology also allowed for a new lightness of construction and an airy brightness to enter the churches. This new style became known as gothic and it was about this time that the church took on the cross-shape we see today, and although other shapes and forms were experimented with during the Renaissance, the cross-shape has consistently remained the most popular.

Architectural Styles

GLOSSARY

Avatar	earthly manifestation of a deity
Bai sema	boundary stone to mark consecrated ground
Ban	house or village
Benjarong	Polychromatic ceramics made in China for the Thai market, (lit. five colours)
Bodhisattva	in Mahayana Buddhism, an enlightened being
Bot	main sanctuary in a temple
Brahma	one of the Hindu Trinity: the Creator
Chedi	reliquary tower in Buddhist temple
Cupola	small dome
Dharma	the teachings or doctrine of the Buddha
Dharamchakra	Buddhist Wheel of Law
Erawan	mythical three-headed elephant: Indra's vehicle
Farang	foreign, Western, a foreigner from the West
Feng shui	the art of placing a building or object in its surroundings to benefit the user
Ganesh	Hindu elephant-headed deity
Garuda	mythical Hindu creature: half-man, half-bird: Vishnu's vehicle
Hanuman	Monkey god
Hti	small, sacred umbrellas on the tops of spires.
Indra	Hindu king of the gods
Jataka	stories of the 500 hundred lives of the Buddha
Khlong	canal
Khon	classical dance-drama
Khun	Mr, Mrs, Ms
Kinnari	mythical creature: half-woman, half-bird
Lakhon	classical dance-drama
Lak muang	city pillar, revered home for the city's guardian spirit

Meru	mythical mountain home of the gods in Hindu and Buddhist cosmologies
Mondop	small, square temple building to house minor images
Muay Thai	Thai boxing
Naga	mythical dragon-headed serpent in Buddhism and Hinduism
Nirvana	final liberation from the cycle of rebirths, state of non-being
Prang	central tower in a Khmer temple
Rama	king of the Chakri dynasty. Human manifestation of Hindu deity Vishnu
Ramayana	Hindu epic of good versus evil
Romanesque	architectural style in Europe from the 7th to the 12th centuries characterised by round-arched openings and heavy stone carving
Sanskrit	sacred language of Hinduism, also used in Buddhism
Shiva	one of the Hindu Trinity: the Destroyer
Soi	lane
Songkhran	Thai New Year (in April)
Takraw	game played with a rattan ball
Tha	pier
Thanon	road
Theravada	main school of Buddhist faith in Thailand
Tripitaka	Buddhist scriptures
Uma	Shiva's consort
Vishnu	one of the Hindu Trinity: the Preserver
Wai	Thai gesture of greeting and thanks
Wat	temple
Wihan	temple assembly hall for the laity

Glossary

A Note on Language

Whereas most Thais who are used to dealing with foreigners speak some English, you'll delight them if you at least try to make the effort to speak a few words. Thai is a tonal language with five different tones: low, middle, high, rising and falling; this means that the same word can have up to five different meanings depending on the tone used.

Thai is also very monosyllabic and staccato-sounding, so if you're a Westerner you'll have to suppress the urge to infuse emotion into what you're saying in Thai, it will only confuse matters.

You should also try to end your sentences with the word 'krap' if you're a male and 'kaa' if you're a female, it's considered polite; and don't let laughter at your efforts to speak the language put you off, amusement is often nothing more than the Thai way of showing their appreciation for your efforts.

Street signs in Bangkok are almost always written in Roman script as well as Thai, but the English translations can be very inconsistent, so be careful if you need to ask for directions, what you read may not be the actual pronunciation in Thai.

Some Useful Thai

Conversation

Hello	*sa wah dee*
How are you?	*pen yan gai?*
I'm fine	*sa bai dee*
Do you speak English?	*poot angrit?*
I can't speak Thai	*poot thai mai dai*
I don't know	*mai roo*
I understand	*kao jai*
I don't understand	*mai kao jai*
It doesn't matter	*mai pen rai*
Yes	*chai* or *krap* (male) *kaa* (female)
No	*mai chai*
Please	*kor*
Thank you	*kap khun*
No, thank you	*mai aow kap khun*
Sorry	*kor towt*

Directions

Here	*tee nee*
There	*tee nun*
What?	*a rai?*
Why?	*tum mai?*
Where?	*tee nai?*
How?	*yang rai?*
How far?	*kiai tao rai?*
How long?	*nan tao rai?*
How much?	*tao rai?*
Good	*dee*
Bad	*mai dee*
Open	*bpert*
Closed	*bpit*
Left	*sai*
Right	*kwah*
Straight on	*yoo drong nah*
Between	*ra wahng*
On the corner of	*drong hooa moom*
Near	*glai* (falling tone)
Far	*glai* (mid tone)
Up	*keun*
Down	*long*
Entrance	*tahng kao*
Exit	*tahng ork*
Ticket	*tua*
Free	*free*
	(i.e. no charge)
Toilet	*horng nahm*
Temple	*wat*
Market	*ta lat*
Museum	*pi pit ta pun*
Palace	*wang*
Park	*suan*
Road	*ta non*
Lane	*soi*
River	*meh nam*
Canal	*khlong*
Bridge	*sap han*
Boat	*ria*
Ferry	*ria doi sam*
Pier	*ta*
Train	*rot fai*
Taxi	*tak si*

Numbers

0	*soon*
1	*neung*
2	*song*
3	*sahm*
4	*see*
5	*hah*
6	*hok*
7	*jet*
8	*bpairt*
9	*gao*
10	*sip*
11	*sip et*
12	*sip song*
13	*sip sahm*
14	*sip see*
15	*sip hah*
16	*sip hok*
17	*sip jet*
18	*sip bpairt*
19	*sip gao*
20	*yee sip*
21	*yee sip et*
22	*yee sip song*
30	*sahm sip*
40	*see sip*
50	*hah sip*
60	*hok sip*
70	*jet sip*
80	*bpairt sip*
90	*jao sip*
100	*neung roi*
101	*roi et*
200	*song roi*
1,000	*neung pun*

Glossary

LISTINGS

GENERAL
Tourism Authority of Thailand
www.tat.or.th

WALKS
PRATUNAM
Jim Thompson's House
www.jimthompsonhouse.org

Bangkok Art and Culture Centre
www.bacc.or.th

Siam Ocean World
www.siamoceanworld.com

WIRELESS ROAD
Swissotel Nai Lert Park
www.swissotel.com

Central Embassy
www.centralembassy.com

Dusit Thani Hotel
www.dusit.com

SILOM ROAD
Sukhothai Hotel
Tel: 287 0222
www.sukhothai.com

Westin Banyan Tree Hotel
www.banyantree.com

Metropolitan Hotel
www.metropolitan.como.bz

Jim Thompson's Thai Silk Company
www.jimthompson.com

Snake Farm
Tel: 252 0161-4

Neilson-Hays Library
www.neilsonhayslibrary.com

Silom Village Trade Centre
www.silomvillage.co.th

Silom Galleria
www.thesilomgalleria.com

CHAROEN KRUNG ROAD
Oriental Hotel
www.mandarinoriental.com

Royal Orchid Sheraton Hotel
www.royalorchidsheraton.com

River City
www.rivercity.co.th

RATTANAKOSIN
Wat Pho Massage School
www.watphomassage.com

Grand Palace
www.palaces.0thai.net

National Theatre (box office)
Tel: 221 0171

BANG LAMPHOO
Queen's Gallery
www.queengallery.org/en

DUSIT DISTRICT
Vimarnmek Palace
www.thai.palaces.net

Dusit Zoo
www.dusitzoo.org

FURTHER AFIELD
Wat Arun
www.watarun.org

Siam Society
www.siam-society.org

Suan Pakkad Palace
www.suanpakkad.com

LIST OF ILLUSTRATIONS

List of Illustrations

LIST OF MAPS

LIST OF ICONS

Must See
Pages: 18, 24, 25, 38, 50, 61, 76, 86, 91, 99, 106, 112, 116, 126, 133, 138, 143, 144.

National Monument
Pages: 18, 22, 23, 46, 52, 54, 55, 60, 61, 62, 65, 66, 75, 78, 86, 88, 91, 99, 108, 110, 112, 114, 126, 129, 131, 133, 138, 140, 141, 143.

Good View
Pages: 25, 44, 95, 99, 112.

See At Night
Pages: 50, 54, 76, 116.

Drinking
Pages: 21, 32, 44, 50, 55, 61, 76, 116.

Eating
Pages: 21, 25, 32, 44, 50, 55, 61, 76, 116, 129, 144.

Shopping
Pages: 18, 21, 44, 48, 50, 55, 60, 61, 76, 78, 80, 82, 97, 116, 123, 144.

Index

INDEX

Index

NOTES